GIRLS IN THE MIDDLE

Working to Succeed in School

Commissioned by the
AAUW Educational Foundation

Researched and written by
Research for Action, Inc.
Jody Cohen and Sukey Blanc with Jolley Christman, Diane Brown, and Michele Sims

Published by the
American Association of University Women Educational Foundation
1111 Sixteenth Street N.W.
Washington, DC 20036-4873
202/728-7602
http://www.aauw.org
e-mail: info@mail.aauw.org

First printing August 1996 (19,000 copies)

Book design by Adam T. Hong
Woodblock design by Thorina Rose

Cohen, Jody, 1952-
    Girls in the middle : working to succeed in school / by Jody Cohen and Sukey Blanc
with Jolley Christman ... [et al.] ; Research for Action.
        p.   cm.
    Includes bibliographical references and index.
    ISBN 1-879922-15-0 (soft cover)
    1. Women—Education (Secondary)—United States. 2. Sex discrimination in
education—United States. 3. Sex differences in education—United States. 4. Middle
school students—United States. 5. Educational surveys—United States.   I. Blanc, Sukey,
1953- . II. Research for Action (Organization : Philadelphia, Pa.) III. American Association
of University Women. Educational Foundation. IV. Title.
LC1755.C65   1996
376′ .63′0973—dc20   96-24677

The AAUW Educational Foundation extends its grateful appreciation to Ruth and John Jurenko for their generous support of Girls in the Middle.

The AAUW Educational Foundation provides funds to advance education, research, and self-development for women, and to foster equity and positive societal change.

In principle and practice, the AAUW Educational Foundation values and supports diversity. There shall be no barriers to full participation in this organization on the basis of gender, race, creed, age, sexual orientation, national origin, or disability.

CONTENTS

Tables

Girls in the Middle: Working to Succeed in School is the third of three reports in the American Association of University Women Educational Foundation's research series on what is working for girls in school. In addition to offering readers an incisive look at how adolescent girls experience middle school and achieve, it provides a new understanding of how schools use various educational reforms to foster an equitable climate for student achievement.

Girls in the Middle takes the reader inside the developmental laboratory we call middle school for a close-up look at the critical choices girls make in their daily school lives. By design, the report looks not at some composite called "all girls," but at very individual girls making choices in highly complex situations. It looks at girls who differ in race, ethnicity, and demography—whether urban, rural, or suburban—and broadens the definition of girls' success by considering a range of successes—academic, social, artistic, and athletic. By illuminating the many pressures on girls of this age and the strategies girls use to achieve, Girls in the Middle challenges assumptions about girls' behaviors and about school programs and policies designed to foster growth.

The middle school focus is also deliberate. The Foundation recognizes that middle school is a pivotal stage for all students—a stage in which personal and educational decisions can have far-reaching effects. That others concur is evidenced by the influential reports of the Carnegie Council on Adolescent Development (Turning Points, A Matter of Time, Great Transitions) and the recent rash of attention on middle school curricula and teaching structures. Girls in the Middle expands the scope of this inquiry by highlighting gender issues as they are affected by school reform.

Why a gender focus? To make visible the invisible, to bridge a major societal divide. Thirteen years ago, the U.S. Department of Education set off public alarms when A Nation At Risk, its scathing report on the nation's public schools, decried "a rising tide of mediocrity that threatens our very future." A flood of reports, studies, and recommendations followed in the report's wake. But not until the landmark 1992 publication of The AAUW Report: How Schools Shortchange Girls did the recommendations take gender into account. Like its forerunner, Girls in the Middle promises to preserve gender equity's place in national discussions on educational reform.

With *Girls in the Middle*, the Foundation completes its Positive School Climate research series. The other two reports in the series, also funded by the Foundation's Eleanor Roosevelt Fund for Women and Girls, are a literature review and a data analysis. The literature review, *Growing Smart: What's Working for Girls in School* (1995), surveys learning approaches that foster girls' achievement and healthy development. The data analysis, *The Influence of School Climate on Gender Differences in the Achievement and Engagement of Young Adolescents*, examines how well school climate factors measured in the U.S. Department of Education's National Education Longitudinal Study (NELS:88) contribute to gender equity.

Together, the three reports provide new insights about girls from three different perspectives. The richness of the combined research and the range of research methods employed should make the reports valuable to all educational leaders and policymakers.

By making young people's lives visible, the Foundation hopes that *Girls in the Middle* will help school and community adults recognize girls as active agents with distinct styles and strategies for achievement. We feel confident that acknowledging these strategies and using school reforms to expand the range of roles open to all students will create new possibilities for girls' success and achievement.

Alice Ann Leidel
President
AAUW Educational Foundation
August 1996

T his report was prepared by Research for Action, Inc., under a contract with the American Association of University Women Educational Foundation. Adults and youngsters in six schools gave generously of their time, energy, and insight to make this study happen.

While two of us, Jody Cohen and Sukey Blanc, were primarily responsible for writing the report, we are very appreciative of the contributions of our compatriot researchers Alisa Belzer, Diane Brown, Jolley Bruce Christman, Bonnie Mason, Joan McCreary, and Michele Sims. They not only spent weeks in the field documenting what they saw and heard, but also contributed their invaluable insights at research team meetings and in countless other conversations. Diane, Jolley, and Michele also wrote sections of several chapters. Our collaborative work relationships at Research for Action and our perspectives on student and practitioner research provided a backdrop and continually informed this effort.

Consultants both formal and informal were also critical to the making of this report. Sari Biklen served throughout to help us design the study and frame what we were learning; she helped us to stay with the girls' perspectives. Aida Nevarez provided valuable insights into issues of race and culture for girls in schools. Pat Macpherson brought in-depth knowledge of the literature on adolescent girls, deep familiarity with issues of gender and reform in secondary schools, and consistent attention to our data as they unfolded. Shirley Brown and Annette Lareau generously gave of their time and insights on early drafts. Rachel Martin helped us gain access to a site and knowledge of a culture and worked with our student researchers when we left town. Gary Anderson, Katherine Herr, and Michelle Fine assisted at critical moments with access, consultations on research as pedagogy, and ethical advice. Katherine Mooney entered at a critical moment to help us understand what we were trying to say and then say it; we hope her intelligence, rigor, and humor are woven into the report.

Renee Jones and Cameron Voss played crucial roles: Renee took care of the logistics that kept the research team moving. Cameron was invaluable in helping us pull the final draft together and solving last minute glitches. Both helped us all to stay sane.

At the AAUW Educational Foundation Priscilla Little, Tanya Hilton, Judy Markoe, Gabrielle Lange, and Wabei Siyolwe were generous with their time, energy, and insights. We're appreciative of their respect for our sometimes messy process as qualitative researchers. Susan Morse was a wonderful editor, gentle and sharp at the same time.

Finally, our families—David Dan, Jesse Cohen-Dan, and Lucas Cohen Dan, and Paul Socolar, Robin Blanc and Elena Blanc—gave us throughout their intelligences as well as their support and love.

Thanks!

CHAPTER ONE

NEW CHALLENGES, NEW EXPECTATIONS

While the women's movement has given many girls more options than they've had in the past, and a shifting economy has increased the pressure on women to boost their incomes, girls still move toward adulthood in a society that continues to denigrate women, especially women of color.[1] In their middle school years, girls are expected to adopt new female roles demanded by a rapidly changing employment picture while simultaneously handling the sudden physiological and psychological changes associated with puberty.[2]

This report is about girls in their middle school years. It looks at the ways girls negotiate school, as seen through the eyes of "insiders"—students, school staff, administrators, and parents—so as to explore how school can work better for girls. It also gauges girls' reactions, where possible, to gender equity initiatives and school reform efforts, present to varying degrees in all the schools studied. As we met and talked with young adolescent girls of diverse backgrounds and abilities, we found that despite their differences all were struggling with changing social circumstances and ideas about gender and an often contradictory set of expectations for females. Adolescent girls are to be sexy and flirtatious but at the same time to remain "good girls." They are to fend off aggressive male attention while simultaneously meeting teachers' expectations of nonaggressive behavior. Females are to put domestic life first at the same time that they prepare for financial independence.

Middle schools are in a position to empower girls encountering such challenges through educational reforms that address issues of gender equity. However, the literature on middle schools[3] and female development[4] offers us little about how schools might incorporate gender equity into reform. In this study we set out to find schools meeting with some measure of success in just that challenge. We bring back reports from the field that shed light on how schools can weave gender equity into educational reform at the levels of policy, program, and individuals.

Why This Study Now

This qualitative study builds on the findings of a recent surge of research on how schools are "shortchanging" girls. Research conducted over the last decade has used surveys administered to thousands of youngsters[5] and observations of hundreds of schools and thousands of classrooms[6] to support such findings as these: Across the nation, often well-meaning teachers continue to deliver subtle but powerful messages reinforcing boys' dominance in the classroom. Curricula continue to reflect inequities, as materials by and about women remain peripheral and teaching approaches continue to favor predominantly male interactional styles. Girls' self-esteem and confidence in their competence, particularly with regard to math and science, drop precipitously during their middle school years, narrowing their later choices of course work and career path.

Adolescent girls struggle with an often contradictory set of expectations. They are to be sexy and flirtatious but at the same time remain "good girls." They are to fend off aggressive male attention while simultaneously meeting teachers' expectations of nonaggressive behavior. Females are to put domestic life first at the same time that they prepare for financial independence.

These studies hold devastating implications—for young women as well as for schools and society, which will not realize the talents of half the population. The broad-based studies examine large numbers of girls and schools to reach their conclusions. However, a picture of girls as individual agents making meaning and choices is almost absent from these studies. Likewise missing are fully contextualized pictures of particular schools as institutions that host as well as resist change. Writer Peggy Orenstein's reports on adolescent girls in two California schools begin to put real faces on the broad findings.[7] Rich, textured pictures of diverse girls and schools across the country are critical to designing policies and programs that will support gender awareness and equity in education. In instances where schools and teachers have initiated overt and often easy efforts, greater equity has resulted, as evident for example in girls' rising math scores.[8] In this study we set out to examine and document such instances.

In this exploratory study that builds on the work of *The AAUW Report: How Schools Shortchange Girls* and *Growing Smart: What's Working for Girls in School,*[9] we invite readers into the perspectives and experiences of girls and the middle schools they enter daily. Although the names of schools and people in those schools have been changed to preserve their anonymity, quotes are actual and individual. In the midst of education that "shortchanges" and "fails" girls, we look for exceptions—girls who are negotiating these challenging years successfully and schools that are employing strategies that support girls—to discover what they might teach us about educating all girls.

The ways girls negotiate their school lives highlight their active struggles to make sense of their complex worlds. Adolescent girls are always negotiating their lives—perceiving circumstances, weighing options, making and revising choices. By looking at girls' strategies of negotiation, this report illuminates the ways that adolescent girls change their approaches and personae in response to external circumstances and internal promptings.

Finding what works for girls requires broadening the scope of inquiry to include such factors as school reform and home and peer cultures. First, we must grapple with outcomes: What do we want for girls? Our reading of the literature on adolescent girls[10] in tandem with our research in middle schools suggests this answer: Girls should be recognized by adults and taught to recognize themselves as complex individuals with an emerging vision, an ability to think critically, a sense of entitlement to giving voice and being heard, and a range of choices about who they are and want to become.

Rather than favoring girls who exhibit one kind of strength over another, this outcome would recognize a broad repertoire of possible strengths and achievements—a range of ways in which girls might be successful. The desired outcome would validate achievement in school on a continuum that would recognize both the girl struggling to learn and the honors student using her good grades to pursue a next ambition. It would validate girls who may not be achieving conventional success—that is, getting good grades—but are evidencing success in other venues such as athletics or peer leadership.

Finally, we cannot look at outcomes for girls without also reconsidering boys' opportunities and challenges. Efforts to promote equity and empowerment of all students must take on boys' issues related to gender as well as issues between boys and girls.[11] Like girls, adolescent boys face restrictive gender stereotypes. They are pressured to be tough and not vulnerable, for example. But those who are too physically intimidating may be branded troublemakers and face an increased risk of special education placement, a problem for African American boys in particular. Both girls and boys need change strategies that will decrease antagonism and support cooperation and respect between the genders. Strategies for enhancing the education of girls complement and even overlap strategies for enriching boys' options.[12]

This report speaks with multiple voices—the voices of girls and also those of their teachers and parents, counselors and school nurses, administrators, aides, and male peers. Each brings her or his own partial perspectives—coming from her or his age, position, gender, race/ethnicity, social class, and history.[13] Our intent is not to reach consensus on a single truth about what works for girls in schools but rather to describe the dynamic relationship between girls and their school contexts and to draw implications for gender equity and school reform.

A Way of Looking

To learn how girls negotiate middle school, we draw on the qualitative research methods of participant observation, interviewing, and document analysis used by anthropologists and sociologists to study how groups of people think and behave. Qualitative researchers observe, participate in a setting, and ask questions in order to illuminate the meanings of people's daily interactions. They systematically document what they see and hear, using this data to generate and test the validity of their hypotheses. (For further discussion of methodology, see Appendix A.) This approach is helpful in understanding the experiences of girls in middle school for two reasons. First, it reveals contextual factors that shape school climate as well as the values, attitudes, and beliefs that underlie people's interaction.[14] Second, qualitative research can uncover previously hidden aspects of gendered experiences in school.[15]

The vignette below, taken from a researcher's field notes, illustrates what we can learn from systematic looking and listening. The notes describe a classroom scene in a course on Family and Consumer Sciences. We follow a student named Norma as she takes part in both the formal curriculum (the intended instructional content) and the informal curriculum created by teacher and students as they interact over time in the setting.[16] By observing Norma in the context of her classroom, we can gain insight into school culture and its relationship to individual girls.

> The room has the warm, pungent smell of dough sizzling in cooking oil. Twenty eighth graders—male and female, Hispanic, Native American, and Anglo—hover over bread boards and cast-iron frying pans. Norma, a large, serious girl described by a teacher as "more worldly, different" from her peers in this rural setting, has rushed for her apron. Now she scoops and sprinkles flour for lithe, chattering Raina. Raina kneads the flour into the dough as she and Norma chat and laugh. Don stands over the fry pan, interrupting frequently for more of the donut-shaped dough. He pokes Raina. Norma flips a dish towel at him and tells him, "Stop it!" "Hey babe," he menaces back with a loose fist.
>
> Mrs. Perez, their teacher, runs her index finger across the floury counter surface and nods. "Do you know, they still call me 'babe' at home even at fifty-one!"
>
> Raina pipes up, "You look younger than that."
>
> Mrs. Perez smiles—"You get an A!"—then continues in a reflective tone. "You know, I had a teacher in high school—the boys told her she looked pretty and they all got A's. The girls got B's. Don't worry. I won't do that to you."
>
> Don cranes his neck to keep an eye on both browning donuts and Mrs. Perez's creased, smiling face. "Why not? Sounds good!"
>
> Minutes later, kids have set the tables and are snacking in their cooking groups with evident pride and pleasure. Don has set their group's table, Norma empties a pan of donuts into a napkinned basket. As we bite into warm donuts, Mrs. Perez tells me, "They're socializing and that's important too. We're wrong when we try to leave that out of school."
>
> (From a researcher's fieldnotes, 2/1/95)

Social interaction and learning are both evident in this classroom. Norma, who is self-conscious with peers about her large, developing body as well as her strong academic work, picks up on a structured opportunity to interact with the socially adept Raina. Norma even finds the environment safe enough to assert herself with a boy. It is also safe enough to create a "teachable moment" for Ms. Perez, who, by volunteering a personal story, opens a public discussion on issues of gender and power that simmer beneath the surface of classroom banter.

Part of a teacher's skill in such interactions lies in knowing which student comments to probe and which to let slide. Here, Ms. Perez chooses not to make an issue of Don's use of the term "babe," and so avoids jeopardizing the comfortable tone of the exchange.

This scene—interpreted with the aid of further observations and interviews with Norma, Don, and Ms. Perez—helps us understand the code of beliefs and behaviors that participants bring to this classroom. It also tells us something about the prevailing assumptions and mores of a school culture. For instance, the class setting is one traditionally viewed as female. These eighth graders still refer to it as Home Ec. though the teacher uses the statewide course title Family and Consumer Sciences. Girls' traditional roles and competence are implicitly acknowledged here, but both girls and boys are actually doing the cooking.

Collecting and layering these multiple dimensions of information is the researcher's task. The depth of the combined information can tell more about girls' status in school than standard indices of success such as test scores and grades taken out of the context of girls' lives. By using the same technique to look systematically at a school's many formal and informal activities, we can extrapolate themes and patterns that reveal what is going on for girls across the school.

In this report, we will move back and forth between individuals and their contexts to uncover how girls negotiate school and how schools take up issues of equity and educational reform that support girls. By considering gender equity as it fits with other school reform, we will show how understanding school culture as well as the cultures that girls themselves construct in school should inform both broad educational reform policy and local efforts to change schools.

What We Did

At the outset of this study, we looked for six middle schools interested in participating in a study on girls in school. We wanted schools that would represent a range of geographic locations as well as urban, suburban, and rural settings. We also wanted schools that would give us many different kinds of girls to talk with and think about in relation to their school settings. To address gaps in a literature that disproportionately references white, middle-class girls and tends to reference other girls in groups identified by race/ethnicity, we wanted to include both schools that represent isolation by such factors as race and class, as for example an urban school with predominantly African American students, and schools that represent the mixed populations of multicultural settings. Overall, the school mix we selected attempts to represent broadly the racial/ethnic mix in schools nationwide. All of our schools are involved with educational reform efforts. For some of the schools, reform has entailed explicit work with gender awareness and equity. (See table of participating schools on page 7.)

Between November 1994 and March 1995, researchers made two visits to each of the six schools selected. We observed dozens of classes and other formal and informal activities, interviewed hundreds of girls in focus groups and individually, and also solicited perspectives from boys, school staff, parents, and community members. We conducted open-ended interviews that provided in-depth insights into the world views, hopes, and dilemmas of individuals, and we collected achievement data on girls identified as "successful." (For a more extended description of our field methodology, including sample observation guides and interview questions, see the appendix.)

Critical to our research approach was the teaming of "outside" researchers with school "insiders." Insiders helped outsiders identify relevant people, places, policies, and programs in the school setting. Together, inside and outside researchers posed and addressed pertinent questions. Our research team was composed of eight women of diverse races and ethnicities, including several secondary teachers. At each school site, two outside researchers worked with at least one adult insider—a teacher—and a group of female students, who acted as both key informants and co-researchers. The girl researchers were selected by adults and student peers to meet criteria of girls evidencing school success in one or more areas including academic achievement, school leadership, peer leadership, creativity, and athletic participation. Working with teachers and students to frame questions, collect data, and build interpretations across different perspectives helped outsiders gain access to local knowledge and illuminated girls' experiences of school.

Outside researchers conducted three-day visits early in the fall of 1994 to begin to develop relationships with insiders, learn about the schools and surrounding communities, identify gender issues, and make contact with community stakeholders, such as school-community liaisons and business- or university-based school partners. Often with their inside contacts, outsiders attended classes, assemblies, faculty meetings, and extracurricular activities, ate lunch with students and teachers, and interviewed students, staff, parents, and community members. (See sample schedule on page 8.) After identifying critical issues, researchers returned to the school sites in mid-winter for a week. At each school, researchers "shadowed" five to eight girls through their school days, interviewing them along with their friends, teachers, and parents to gain a deeper understanding of the multiple spheres these girls negotiate.

Middle Schools Participating in Study

SCHOOL	SETTING	LOCATION	SIZE	RACE/ETHNICITY	CLASS	GENDER INITIATIVES	REFORM EFFORTS
Garth	Urban	East Coast	1,300	98% African American 2% Latino	87% qualify for AFDC	Teacher inquiry seminar Girls' groups	Peer mediation Leadership committee Small learning communities
Parkside	Urban	East Coast	750	41% Latino 13% Asian 22% White 22% African American 2% Middle Eastern	86% of students live on or below the poverty level	Girls' group "No put down" policy	Shared decision-making Portfolio assessment Staff development on cooperative learning Culturally sensitive curriculum
Madison	Suburban	Midwest	800	80% White 10% African American 4% Asian 4% Latino	Predominantly middle class	Sexual harassment policy Staff development on gender equity	Restructuring into teams Inclusion of special needs students
Valley Stream	Suburban	West Coast	1,030	70% White 22% Latino 4% Asian 2% African American 2% other	206 on free lunch 77 on reduced-cost lunch	Lunchtime girls' rap group All-girls math class Sexual harassment policy	Team teaching Grade level themes Block scheduling Middle school math renewal Peer mediation
Avila	Rural	Southwest	500	45% Latino 45% Native American 10% White	Poor, working class A few middle class Many pueblo residents and welfare recipients	None explicit	Thematic strands Active teaching and learning approaches Multicultural curriculum Site-based management
Fairfield	Rural	Southeast	525	70% White 30% African American	Ranges from poor to well-to-do	None explicit	Small learning communities Block scheduling Adviser period daily Homework support program

Sample Schedule for Three-Day School Visit

Before their initial visits, researchers asked their school contacts to help them devise a schedule that would make the best use of researchers' limited school time. Researchers sent schools a sample schedule to indicate the range of people, places, and events they hoped to encounter and the pace they could keep. During the visit, researchers found these schedules very helpful in establishing an overview of their setting and connections with key girls and adults in the schools. At least two researchers took part in every site visit.

DAY 1	Researcher #1	Researcher #2
Period 1	Focus group with student-researchers	
Period 2	Interview teacher-researcher(s)	Observe class
Period 3	Observe class	Interview principal
Period 4	Hang out with students at lunch	Hang out with staff at lunch
Periods 5 & 6	Talk with nurse, counselor, other adults in school	Focus group with 6 - 8 girls
After school	Focus group with staff interested in gender issues	

DAY 2	Researcher #1	Researcher #2
Periods 1 & 2	Shadow student through the day	Observe class/activity
Period 3		Focus group with 6 - 8 girls (new group)
Period 4		Join staff at lunch
Periods 5 & 6		Talk with parents and other community stakeholders
		Arrange for next visit

DAY 3	Researcher #1	Researcher #2
Periods 1 & 2	Meet with student-researchers	Shadow student through day
Period 3	Meet with teacher-researcher(s)	
Periods 4 - 6	Talk with students and adults to set up next visit	

What We Found

This report does not offer a recipe—a list of reforms that work for all girls. Rather, it makes evident the impossibility of such a list. This is so because girls are individuals negotiating disparate schools, and because schools likewise must manage contexts that encourage some actions and discourage others. Girls and schools are engaged in a complicated and dynamic relationship. What this exploratory study does indicate is that girls employ a range of strategies in their efforts to succeed at school; that urban, suburban, and rural middle schools pose distinctive challenges and opportunities for meeting the goal of gender equity; and that meshing gender equity with middle school reform requires coordinating efforts at the levels of policy, program, and invested individuals. (See Chapter Five for a fuller discussion of outcomes.)

Middle school girls approach the challenges and opportunities of their school environments by drawing on one of several sets of strengths and strategies. Whether or not a girl's strategy is deemed "successful" is a function of the interplay between the girl and her school context.

The Research for Action team set out in search of school reforms that work for girls. What we found was a startling diversity of girls whose different constructions of self and school made problematic the notion of what we meant by "working" and who we meant by "girls." As we analyzed our cross-site data on young adolescent girls, we discovered that in all of our schools and across such identity categories as race/ethnicity and class, girls tended to approach the challenges and opportunities of their school environments by drawing on one of several sets of strengths and strategies. Whether or not a girl employing a particular set of negotiating strategies was deemed "successful" in her school was a function of the interplay between the girl and her school context. For example, a girl who spoke her mind might be seen in one setting as stimulating those around her while in another as having "an attitude."

Identifying girls as agents who negotiate school differently suggests that the more fertile a school in terms of opportunities, role models, and recognition for a wide range of female behaviors and achievements, the more apt are girls to flourish. Given this, our own desired outcome had to headline the importance of choices and entitlement: Girls had to be able to envision a wide repertoire of possibilities including the traditionally female. They had to be able to develop skills as critical readers of the cultures they inhabit. They had to be able to feel entitled to act in order to risk becoming themselves. By looking at how individual girls respond to reform, we can begin to envision what educational equity might look like for all girls.

Like girls, parents and teachers are struggling with shifting circumstances. Across their differences, many of these adults are doing their best to provide girls and boys with equal educational opportunities. Boys, too, acknowledge a changing environment. As one put it, "[My parents] are pretty much teaching me to be equal. It's pretty much that society has changed so much so it's like you're kind of used to it by now." However, school cultures—evident in policies, programs, and behaviors—are nowhere entirely consistent with the educational beliefs and stated ideas of members of the larger school community. It is critical that schools help adults and youngsters come together to make sense of conflicting pressures. Such use of public spaces fertilizes real change.

The Plan of the Report

This report begins with the girls themselves. The second chapter lays out the typology of strategies girls use to negotiate school. Then it presents six girls—one from each of the six school sites—who demonstrate the range of this typology. The reader will come to understand the typology better by getting to know these girls through their own voices, the voices of people important in their lives, and researchers' field notes and analyses. The chapter argues that girls are active agents making choices about how they approach their school lives. Their success in school depends in part on how their approaches work in their particular settings.

In the third chapter we look more closely inside three middle schools from the sometimes contrasting perspectives of girls identified as successful and adults who play important roles as mentors and/or authorities. This case study approach offers readers the opportunity to view these schools "from the inside," learning about middle school reforms and gender equity initiatives as experienced by participants. The chapter highlights the somewhat distinctive strengths and challenges of suburban, urban, and rural schools in terms of promoting gender equity. It suggests that policies supporting gender equity, the use of school-based adults as mentors, and programmatic middle school reform all contribute to girls' school success.

In Chapter Four we shift perspectives to look at gender issues not girl by girl, or school by school, but through the lens of institutional change. Here we see how schools as organizations situated in particular communities can take on the challenge of working with diverse constituencies to promote gender equity. The chapter suggests that efforts must converge at the levels of policy, programmatic reform, and invested individuals in order for schools to sustain deep changes in institutional culture.

The fifth chapter presents the outcomes and recommendations from this study. These are intended for a broad audience of people who care about our daughters' and sons' educations. As this and other studies suggest, what empowers girls tends also to empower boys. Reform strategies such as detracking, creating small learning communities that afford close relationships among youngsters and adults, devising developmentally appropriate approaches to grade passage and curriculum, and designing multicultural and feminist curricula are approaches that support the learning of all students. Chapter Five lays out recommendations accompanied by sample actions to suggest ways to use this research as a springboard to action.

Policies on educational reform and gender equity in schools have the formidable task of creating avenues to improve schools for all constituent groups—students, parents, administrators, and staff. Policymakers are adults, often males, and often at considerable remove from daily life in schools. To create educational reform that will be effective in meeting girls' needs, decisionmakers at local as well as national levels must hear from those inside schools and especially from girls about what they experience in school, what they want, and what they have to offer.

CHAPTER TWO

HOW GIRLS NEGOTIATE SCHOOL

In her study of girls and boys in elementary school, Barrie Thorne argues that while adults influence how children take up being female and male, children themselves "act, resist, rework, and create…as social actors in a range of institutions."[17] Likewise, young adolescent girls learn the social patterns of the adult world at the same time that they are actively interpreting the world and shaping their own values. In the face of an onslaught of cultural and personal messages about what it means to be female, their task is monumental. They must both prune and blossom, cope and strategize; they must invent themselves. Girls at this developmental crossroad share a set of challenges as they come to grips with issues of autonomy and connection. They also differ from each other in ways that shape their choices and emerging identities.

Developmental psychologists theorize that while boys are most psychologically at risk in childhood, for girls the time of greatest risk is adolescence.[18] Carol Gilligan and her colleagues track preadolescent girls who are resilient, lively, willful, courageous, and honest through their early adolescence. Then these same girls begin peppering their speech with "I don't know," signaling what these researchers describe as "a giving up of voice, an abandonment of self, for the sake of becoming a good girl and having relationships."[19] While some girls respond to the developmental crisis of adolescence by "devaluing themselves and feeling themselves to be worthless…others disagree publicly and dissociate themselves from institutions which devalue them—in this case, the schools."[20]

Much of the early research conducted by Gilligan and her colleagues has been with middle- and upper-middle-class white girls. Researchers focusing on the challenges for young adolescent girls of color have noted that these girls "are making this passage embedded within a family and a community that is most often negatively impacted by a sociopolitical context framed by racial, gender, and economic oppression."[21] Writing about Native American preadolescents, Ardy Bowker notes that their development is shaped by their early initiation into "adult problems and adult responsibilities."[22] Tracy Robinson and Janie Ward argue that the young woman of color must be taught "resistance that will provide her with the necessary tools to think critically about herself, the world, and her place in it."[23]

Three Behavioral Strategies

As our researchers talked with young adolescent girls across the country, we heard girls' accounts of the pressures to be "nice" and quiet, to get along with everyone, to avoid conflict or even notice. But we also heard girls describe themselves with pride as having a "loud voice," being tall, being willing to stand up for their beliefs. These girls were active agents using an amalgamation of strategies to negotiate their school days. In this chapter we describe three strategic approaches that we saw used by girls identified as "successful" in school. We call these approaches "speaking out," "doing school," and "crossing borders," terms we coined to describe what we saw.

Speaking Out. Some girls tend to assert themselves, speaking out and insisting on being heard in both friendly and unfriendly circumstances. This is an approach often used by a girl with a strong sense of herself, her identity, her ideas, and her place in the hierarchies of school and peer cultures. A girl using this strategy may describe herself and be described by peers as "not afraid to say what she thinks."

Across our research sites, some girls habitually speak out. They make themselves highly visible in their schools and become "maverick leaders" who are publicly acknowledged. Others become earmarked as "negative leaders" or "troublemakers," youngsters with notable potential who risk being tagged for failure unless they can change others' perceptions of them. Whether a girl who speaks out becomes identified by herself and others as a leader or a troublemaker may well have to do with her relationships with key adults and how these adults are positioned in the school. It may also have to do with how well her home and community cultures match the dominant culture of the school.

Doing School. Some girls behave in ways that have been traditionally expected of them in school, doing what is asked and speaking in turn, if at all. This approach, too, can be seen as two sides of a coin, as girls call up traditional "good girl" ways of negotiating school either with apparent comfort or to cover dimensions of who they are.

The "schoolgirl" who employs such commonly agreed-upon strategies for success as doing her work on time, listening, and complying with adults' expectations may experience a comfortable fit between her home persona and school culture. Her worlds may well overlap, minimizing daily dissonance. Although she may have put on hold ideas that contradict expected norms, for the time being she has used this strategy to negotiate a viable deal.

A girl who is "playing schoolgirl" employs similar strategies but with greater ambivalence and perhaps even strife. She may be trying to achieve or at least to define her own goals, which may be less congruent with school goals. A girl negotiating school in this way is outwardly compliant and successful in school but leaves clues to her other identity and worlds, which may fit uneasily with school culture. While she is likely to receive adult support in her schoolgirl guise, adults and even peers in the school setting may not be privy to other challenges she is facing. Therefore, she may not be receiving support for the deep work of constructing her own identity.

Girls "doing school" tend to receive adult approval, though perhaps they receive less attention in class than more demanding students. Adults may name them as "good girls" rather than as leaders.

Crossing Borders. Finally, girls who cross borders between different cultures or sets of norms and expectations may achieve success in school and with peers as well as in their home communities, becoming proficient in two or more codes of speech and behavior and gaining stature as "schoolgirls/cool girls." These girls tend to be recognized by adults and peers alike as "successful" and "knowing everybody."

Some of these girls emerge as school leaders who can act as "translators" because of their ability to understand, communicate, and even facilitate others' interactions across disparate worlds, such as school and community, or adults and adolescents. In some settings, border crossers may be recognized in their schools as girls who carry important knowledge, and their schools may call on them to act as "stranger handlers," helping new people enter the cultural sphere of the school. Elsewhere, these girls and their talents may go unrecognized by school authorities, particularly in settings where differences go unacknowledged and strangers are rare.

Girls' approaches align somewhat with their class and/or race—with middle-class and white girls more likely to present as "quiet" and "nice," and working-class girls and girls of color likelier to risk confrontation. Our observations confirm research describing white and black working-class girls as sharing approaches such as a willingness to speak out.[24] However, class and race alone are not necessarily predictive of where a girl falls in this typology. More critical is the match between a girl's own race/ethnicity and class and the dominant culture of her school, which might make a particular strategy feel more available to some girls than to others. For example, a Latina in a school setting where both adults and peers were also predominantly Latino might employ a different strategic approach from a Latina in a predominantly white setting. Additionally, this racial/ethnic match might influence the school's view: For example, a girl regarded as a maverick leader in a school setting where she's of the dominant culture might be viewed as a troublemaker in another, where she's a minority.

In practice, girls' strategic approaches seem sometimes to overlap fully with their identities. As girls assess and select available strategies, at some moments more consciously than others, they may "become" their strategies for periods of time as they sort through options in the process of forming identities. However, their strategic approaches must be distinguished from the girls themselves.

Distinguishing strategies from girls helps us see the ways that some approaches may be precluded and others assisted by environmental factors. Separating approaches from girls' personae also highlights the fact that the same strategies may be interpreted differently at different schools or at different times. Thus, behaviors that evidence "leadership" in one setting, for example, might elsewhere be interpreted as "bullying." Finally, separating strategies from girls allows us to assess opportunities girls have to change their approaches. During their middle school years, girls may try on different strategies like so many coats as part of their self-discovery process. As a boy at one school saw it, girls were "actors," "impostors" who "change instead of staying the same." But rather than indicating falsity, this process of exploration is essential for girls' growth. Understanding girls' experimentation with strategies can help educators re-examine girls' choices in light of their options.

This chapter will use the typology of strategies as a framework to introduce six girls from the study who represent a range of approaches to negotiating school. Like the other girls in this study, these girls were selected because they were deemed "successful." Our criteria for success in school were necessarily complex, given different definitions of success held by disparate cultures within and outside of school. While we looked at such conventional indicators as academic achievement measured by grade and test scores, we also sought the perspectives of adults in school as well as peers and our own research team to identify girls achieving success in a range of ways including academically, athletically, creatively, as school and/or peer leaders, and as reflective observers of their worlds.

Typology of Girls' Strategies for Negotiating School

Speaking Out. Some girls tend to assert themselves, speaking out and insisting on being heard in both friendly and unfriendly circumstances. A girl who speaks out may be perceived as a maverick leader or a troublemaker, depending on her relationships with key adults, the adults' positions in the school, and the degree to which a girl's identity and approach match the dominant culture of the school.

Maverick Leader. Some girls who habitually speak out make themselves highly visible in their schools and become publicly acknowledged as leaders.

Troublemaker. Other girls who also speak out become identified as "negative leaders" with unrealized potential. Girls viewed as troublemakers may increase their risk of failure until they change others' perceptions of them.

Doing School. Some girls conform to traditional expectations of girls in school, doing what is asked and speaking in turn or not at all. Like speaking out, this approach is two-sided, and depending on the girl and her context, can play to girls' advantage or disadvantage.

Schoolgirl. Some girls employ traditional "good girl" ways of negotiating school with apparent comfort, such as doing work on time, listening, and complying with adults' expectations.

Play Schoolgirl. Other girls call up "good girl" behaviors partly to cover up who they really are. This pretense can involve ambivalence and perhaps even strife. Girls using this approach are outwardly compliant and successful in school but leave clues to their other identities and worlds, which may fit uneasily with school culture.

Crossing Borders. Some girls move easily between different cultures or sets of norms and expectations, bridging the gulf, for instance, between peers and adults or between different racial or ethnic groups. These girls are able to move into and out of various settings, taking on characteristics sufficient to "fit" wherever they are. While some maintain separation between their spheres, other border crossers take on the responsibility of "translating" across these different cultures.

Schoolgirl/Cool Girl. Some girls may achieve success in school, with peers, and in their home community, becoming proficient in two or more codes of speech and behavior, thus gaining stature.

Translator. Some girls emerge as school leaders, able to understand and communicate across cultural groups and even facilitate or mediate others' interactions across such divides as school and community, or adults and adolescents.

Our work was complicated by the different ways in which schools interpreted the same strategies, so that what worked in one environment might not work in another. While it is critical to view girls as authors of their identities and agents in their lives, their ongoing interaction with their environments also tempers and shapes who they are becoming. The work was further complicated by shifts in girls' approaches and degree of success even within the period of the research. Within each set of strategies for making sense and making choices, girls may take different paths. For example, a girl who is well liked by peers and also achieves academically may seek low visibility to balance the demands of being both a "schoolgirl" and a "cool girl," or she may choose greater visibility for herself by taking on the work of translating school values for peers while also helping adults to penetrate adolescents' perspectives.

While we began this research looking for successful girls who could help us understand what about their schools worked for them, what we discovered was a richer picture involving a dynamic relationship between girls and schools and greater insight into both the meanings and the fragility of success for adolescent females.

This study is predicated on the notion that both girls and schools change. Historically, girls entering adolescence have been pressured to alter their school personae to fit a relatively narrow definition of success.[25] Research indicates that as young adolescent girls begin to suppress aspects of themselves that seem at odds with models of adult femininity, they may experience a sense of "inner division" symptomatic of a separation between what they know to be true and what they can publicly acknowledge.[26] Our research suggests that we reframe the problem, beginning with the girls themselves as lenses on the institutions they inhabit. Rather than asking girls to cut off limbs to fit the procrustean bed of schools, we ask how girls' needs can become visible and how schools can change to address the learning needs of all girls.

Speaking Out

A Maverick Leader. An African American eighth grader at Garth, a large urban middle school, Keisha is a solidly built girl whose expression behind silver-rimmed glasses shifts quickly from meditative to amused or critical. Her attire—a study in contradictions—may provide clues to her complex persona. On the day she is to be "shadowed," Keisha wears a white sweater with a long black skirt and patent leather shoes with bows. Her hair is tucked up under a purple and yellow Mickey Mouse cap worn with the rim to the back.

In elementary school, Keisha managed to be aggressive while also achieving in school. She recounts, "I used to fight a lot with boys. 'Cause they always like hittin' on girls and they don't think you're supposed to hit them back. So I hit 'em back." Meanwhile, she earned the place of class valedictorian at elementary school graduation and recalls the standing ovation after her speech as a shining moment of success.

The transition to middle school, however, seemed fraught with difficult choices. She describes herself as a "bad girl" in sixth and seventh grades; adults, she says, regarded her as "a firecracker." Still, Keisha knew she was smart and assertive even as she rejected the demands of school. At home her older sister was "running the streets," leaving high school and finally home. Upset about the strife at home and restless in a self-contained classroom with a substitute teacher unable to manage thirty-three sixth graders, Keisha "went wild," fighting and cursing in school and more often than not "cut[ting] out of school and go[ing] to Kentucky Fried Chicken." There were frequent suspensions from school. Nonetheless, Keisha's native intelligence, the same assertiveness that often led her astray of the system, and her connections with several key adults enabled her to pass sixth and seventh grades while friends with whom she cut school were kept back.

As an eighth grader, Keisha is bright, strong, and outspoken, an honor roll student with a math and technology focus. She expresses herself clearly and directly, using so-called Black English or African American Language[27] adeptly to explain her point of view. She explains how she has learned to handle her teacher, Barbara Shane, a white woman with an acerbic style with whom Keisha has had several run-ins. As Keisha describes it, she has had to let her teacher know her abilities and what she can and cannot tolerate. In a reading class where relatively few girls volunteer, Keisha stands out as sharp and alert, both about the subject matter and about how to put herself forward.

> Ms. Shane: Where does the story take place?
> Keisha: Paris. (There is a mild disturbance and Ms. Shane does
> not hear her.)
> Ms. Shane: Carl, the major city in France?
> Carl: Paris.
> Keisha: I said it!
> Ms. Shane: Oh, I'm sorry, I couldn't hear you.

Thereafter, Keisha is called on several times, each time proffering the correct answer, and is also the one to name the opera *Tommy* from yesterday's discussion. She explains to the researcher with scorn that others at her table "don't pay attention in class; that's why they don't know nothing." Later, she is among the first to finish the workbook exercises. For Keisha, this structured and competitive classroom provides a setting where she is developing an academic self and voice. In another setting the teacher might have admonished Keisha for her "attitude," perhaps forfeiting her involvement and her contribution.

Keisha hopes to attend a competitive engineering and science magnet high school in the area. She scored high enough on standardized tests to be placed in eighth-grade algebra. In science, also taught by Ms. Shane, Keisha appreciates the opportunity to take part in active learning that requires collaboration and risk taking, much like doing science in the world: "'We do a lot of experiments and we're not just writing out of the book and having a test next week.... All [the teacher] do is pass out materials. She let us do [the work]. As we grow up, if everybody tell us, then we don't learn to do nothin'."

Keisha negotiates the classroom from the highly visible position of stature and leadership that she has gained at her school. "Everybody knows me. Even people I don't know, know me," she says. This was not always the case. Cutting class and maintaining a reputation as someone not to be "messed with" taught Keisha how and when to raise and lower her visibility. Her self-assured gait and new status as a person of influence seem to guarantee her immunity as she walks through hallways while others are jostled in the crowd or admonished by staff for being in the hall during class.

The new principal, an African American woman who calls Keisha "my miracle baby," met Keisha in the course of hallway confrontations and invited her to join the leadership team she was forming to guide school reform. "I wanted [Keisha] to represent the negative element," the principal explains. This invitation coincided with other factors in Keisha's life to catalyze a change. Keisha describes her role on the reform team as one of knowledge and authority: "It's like having kids there at the meeting to discuss, and we put in our opinion about what should be done about certain things. We know what's goin' on. The teachers [who are not there], we can inform them." While the principal expresses confidence in Keisha's ability "to go on from here, to do whatever it is she wants to do," Keisha in turn acknowledges the valuable currency she has gained by her relationship with the principal.

Keisha credits other adults, mostly African American women, with offering her critical support as well as opportunities to engage in real work. Joann Sellers, a classroom aide in elementary and now in middle school, runs the Performing Arts Club in the community, where Keisha measures her success in terms of her own satisfaction with scripting and performance. Ms. Sellers sees Keisha as making an important contribution to the venture:

"[At the club] Keisha initiated poem writing, 'cause we're doing a calendar as a fundraiser. It focuses on kids in the [club]. She initiated, 'Everybody take your name and come up with things that describe your personality.' I thought it was a great idea [and] the other kids loved it!"

Keisha also describes close relationships with both parents, who offer consistent support and express confidence in her ability to set and achieve her goals.

Invited to participate in this study, Keisha was quick to employ strategies to make herself known to the researchers, to leave her own classes legitimately to conduct research in others' classes, and to help construct the picture of her offered in this report. During an interview she sits erect, smiling slightly and gazing at a filing cabinet as she explains that she wants to be a pediatrician. She likes kids but "never wants to get married because I see how it is with my mom doing all the work in the house."

Information she has gleaned from observing the division of labor in her household influences Keisha's plans for the future.

Keisha has gained a sense of efficacy in school. Working from a solid sense of herself, she sees and takes up opportunities at school. Adults in her reform-minded school as well as adults at home have helped Keisha value and use her strengths. By creating inroads in the school culture and modeling initiative, Keisha in turn helps to foster a climate where students and especially girls take on leadership roles in school reform, sustain meaningful connections with adults, and engage actively in their own learning. On the other hand, Keisha remains willing to break a rule or confront an adult when, as she sees it, the situation warrants.

"Troublemaker." At a middle school in the rural Southwest, a researcher has been shadowing Alicia, a high-achieving Hispanic student. In the scene below, she leaves Alicia and has an encounter with Mona, a Native American youngster whom school staff identified as successful several months earlier. By this second visit, Mona is in trouble and on in-house suspension, spending her days in her advisory teacher's classroom. At lunch she is allowed to join friends.

> In the cafeteria I leave Alicia to her friends and take my tray to one end of a long and otherwise empty table. Suddenly Mona with five of her friends descends on me—smiling gleefully—and settles at my table. As an aide who monitors the lunchroom approaches, I realize that aides are seating students now as a way of maintaining order in the remodeled cafeteria. Mona has astutely used my presence to create a bubble of dissension. The aide directs the girls back to their seats. The others look at Mona, who asserts challengingly, "We're sitting with a teacher!" After several failed efforts to move the girls, the aide insists, "No, you need permission from Mr. Lomas [the principal]!" which I hear as an effort to put an end to it. But Mona has taken off across the crowded cafeteria toward the principal's table and soon returns triumphant, nodding and smiling. "[The principal] said it was okay, ask him." Other students are looking our way now, wavering with their trays. The principal is striding up behind her, apparently figuring out as he approaches that Mona has played us adults against each other. He frowns, shifting gears and telling the girls to return to their places, that I will come sit with them. They retreat amid groans.
>
> (From a researcher's fieldnotes, 1/30/95)

Mona is a slender eighth grader with a coffee-colored complexion, a crooked smile, and straight dark hair that she wears up with tendrils hanging. At the provocation of a familiar lyric, she bursts into rap or laughter.

A Native American living on the Santa Pueblo, Mona embodies some of the tensions of a traditional culture embedded in an insistently modern world. Like many adults on the pueblo, her parents speak *keres*, a native language of the Pueblo Indians, at home. In a school system where English is the official language and Spanish the language of preference and study, the distinction Mona and her friends gain by sharing a secret tongue is offset by their identification as language minority students. The pueblo's economy is dominated by the neon-lit bingo casino, where Mona's older sister works long night hours, often leaving her two-year-old to Mona's care. Mona's mother travels to the city for work as a police dispatcher. From her sister, a single working mom, and her mother who works outside the home and off the reservation, Mona receives information about the economic and domestic pressures on Native American females, whose traditional role is in the home and community.

Apparently comfortable, self-confident, and voluble in a variety of settings, Mona is seen by adults at Avila Middle School as a Native American girl who is atypically unreserved. In a group of girls she quickly stands out, responding readily, singing, laughing, and cursing before the others, as they eye her for behavior cues. But in an interview she admits to feeling alone, distrusting adults at school who "don't understand" or "might phone my dad," being uncomfortable "talking to people [at home]—It is like a weird feeling that grows inside of you when you talk to someone at home," she explains—and, despite a strong peer identification with a girls' gang, feeling unable to open up to other members about deep personal issues because "I don't know how they'd react." Although she is peripherally aware of school personnel such as the counselor and Native American aides designated to support girls like her, Mona does not look to these adults for guidance.

Described by a Native American teaching aide as a girl who showed great promise in the sixth grade, Mona is currently on in-house suspension as a consequence of her behavior in school. Her adviser, a young white woman new to teaching, explains that when she called home to discuss Mona's transgressions, "her mom got angry and told me not to call again. So I sent a registered letter." A conference is necessary to end suspension. The adviser lists Mona's offenses: "She's in big-time trouble. She was brought in by a teacher for screaming obscenities. She chews gum and comes to class late. She also threatened a kid." Like Keisha, Mona possesses intelligence and energy that draw attention to her as "a real leader even when she acts 'bad'...a bright girl making some wrong choices." Unlike Keisha, Mona is described by a teacher as exerting a potent "negative influence on peers"; for key adults, this may take her beyond the possibility of redemption. With regret, her social studies teacher, another white female, notes, "Mona is very smart, very interesting. She's the one I'll remember twenty years from now."

The aide from Mona's pueblo worries that Mona may get expelled: Her grades are poor, her behavior wild, and she shows too much interest in boys. The aide describes the pressures on many pueblo girls to put the community ahead of school:

> If the family is traditional, education is not first on the list.... Women play an important role: They make activities go in the pueblo. They carry it all. Girls grow up knowing what their responsibilities are within the community.... School could take the kids away from the community.

While Mona resists the pressures of school, often not bothering with work that does not interest her, neither does she seem to be complying with expectations in the pueblo, where she "chills" next door, hanging out with an older brother and his friends.

In Mona's home, she is seen as carrying talent and a sense of promise and achievement for the family. She muses on different goals family members hold for her:

> My sister wants me to be a model. My dad wants me to be a singer, 'cause I'm always singing. My brother wants me to be an artist, 'cause I'm like always drawing and everything. But my dad doesn't want me to be a model because I'll be away from home a lot.

She feels that her mother shows her concern by "always trying to straighten me out, like trying to keep me off of drugs, stop smoking, stop drinking. She's just there a lot. She talks to me." Mona's family holds different expectations for her than those typical for the pueblo, and these expectations suggest a more liberal approach to female roles.

Widely acknowledged as a "leader" in the school and particularly among girls, Mona struggles to understand the hazards and potential gains of leadership:

> It's like if you were a young person that no one really paid attention to. And then when you get into a fight it is like you have become popular. Or you are like a queen or something. It is a real good feeling but you got to know when not to get out of hand no matter if anyone tries to pressure you into doing something. It is kind of stupid in a way because people will only be around you 'cause they think that you can protect them. But to me, being a leader is being yourself.

Who is "herself" and can she find and be this self in school? Mona admits, "I don't think of myself [as smart]. I feel like I'm always in trouble," while on the other hand reflecting, "I'm smart. I can do the [work] but I'm too lazy to do it." Though she seems hardly to attend to official classroom agendas, Mona grasps concepts and plugs in relevant information easily. While she sits and reads during suspension, another class begins basic computer programming—learning to create a program and then use it to solve a miles-per-gallon problem. Alicia and her partner are attentive and take notes before getting on the computer. They proceed through the steps but miss a beat. Alicia asks the teacher, "Do I use the dollar sign with miles?" Mona looks up from her book and answers, "No, it's a variable," before focusing again on her lap. A girl who integrates new ideas quickly and can give creative expression to what she sees, Mona would be an excited, exciting student once engaged.

But Mona can name nothing in her school day that engages her energy and creativity except interactions with her boyfriend and the gang. This peer context seems critical. "Once you're involved," she says, "it's very hard to pull out. You lose everything." She pauses, puts three fingers over her heart. "You will have an empty place inside you that you cannot fill."

Reflecting on Girls Who Speak Out. Both Keisha and Mona entered their middle schools as girls who spoke out and were noticed. However, over the three years of middle school, Keisha moved into a position of leadership and centrality at school, whereas Mona increasingly asserted her difference and distance from the adult-defined culture of the school.

Keisha entered middle school exercising "bad girl" strategies that ironically honed her strengths and gained her recognition in the context of a large middle school. She has been supported by critically positioned adults who have encouraged her to define and be herself and have welcomed her voice in shaping core values at her school. The principal as well as a classroom aide familiar with Keisha's home, school, and community worlds have played important roles. An African American young woman at a school that is predominantly African American, Keisha has found a new role for herself with the help of adult mentors attuned to girls' needs, school reform that addresses the needs of girls and boys, and her own strategies.

> Mona can name nothing in her school day that engages her energy and creativity except interactions with her boyfriend and the gang. This peer context seems critical. "Once you're involved," she says, "it's very hard to pull out. You lose everything."

The principal's creation of a leadership team helps Keisha make inquiry work for her. On the leadership team, she says, students "discuss" issues, "know what's going on," and "inform" teachers. This intervention gives students voice and promotes their inquiry into issues of relevance to all members of the school community. Keisha also recognizes this research project as an intervention and positions herself to construct her own portrait for the report.

Keisha employs the strategies of a maverick leader who is savvy and articulate about working the system. She undermines a bureaucratic regime of standardization and control in schools and, by reframing resistance to include often-marginalized voices, she bolsters the idea of school as a site for girls' initiative and leadership. Keisha likes being "good at school." Even so, the fragility of her newfound position is evident considering both her occasional blowups at Garth and the unknowns of her upcoming transition into a large urban high school where she may or may not find opportunities and support.

Like Keisha, Mona is aggressive both verbally and physically, speaking up and flouting norms with apparent ease. Yet school staff as well as peers see her as playing the "troublemaker" or, as a teacher called her, the "negative leader." She entered middle school an extrovert, a youngster whom adults expected to achieve and perhaps even break out of a culture and gender mold that seemed to limit participation for Native American girls. Adults at school continue to name her as a strong, bright, and vocal leader despite the plunge in her grades and her increasing gang involvement. Her peer and home (pueblo) cultures create dissonance with the school culture—and perhaps with each other.

Also, her relationships with adults are not clearing the way for Mona: Her mother is not in regular communication with the school, and the aide from her pueblo has been reluctant to get involved with Mona's "case." Her adviser does not act as her mentor. Mona reminds us that not all school personnel are equally effective with girls and not all girls respond to adult intervention, no matter how skillful or well-intentioned the adult. In any event, it may be that none of these adults is positioned to intercede effectively on Mona's behalf. For Mona, resistance to home and school cultures as defined by adults seems to leave her in the precarious position of defining herself largely in terms of who she is not.

Looking at Keisha and Mona together raises questions about how schools can help girls perceived as troublemakers to reframe their resistance into more constructive channels, perhaps as maverick leaders. With guidance, these energetic and sometimes inspired voices can lend credence to resistance and help schools create avenues of growth for students exhibiting a wide range of talents and sensibilities.

Doing School

A Schoolgirl. Hillary shoots up her hand to put a homework problem on the board. She is a seventh grader, a perky and petite white girl with honey-colored hair. It is third period and this is math—her favorite class.

> I'm good at it. I knew in second grade [that I was good at it]. I could tell then. I got all my sheets right. I always understand when the teacher explains it and lots of times I can figure it out myself. Like multiplying and dividing fractions. I'm real good at that. Geometry is hard for me though and I don't like it.

Hillary's teachers agree with her assessment of herself. This past report card she earned all A's—even in science, her least favorite class because of the "yucky dead things and dirty animals in the classroom." Hillary's literature teacher is very pleased with her work and her contribution to the class: "Hillary is a deep thinker," she says. Hillary returns the compliment: "My literature teacher is my favorite. She's like a mom." The current unit on mythology has caught Hillary's attention: "Myths are like soap operas. I love the stories."

In class Hillary is focused and efficient. She is second to finish an English test and forgoes reading for pleasure or playing a word game with friends in order to get started on the essay assigned for homework. In literature she and her partner quickly translate a poem from dialect to standard English. Her literature teacher explains that this kind of competence and discipline are new for Hillary: "I talked to a teacher from her old school and she told me that Hillary was very silly last year. But she's almost like a little woman this year." This year's Hillary is quite different from last year's as she tries out new strategies and identities in school.

Middle School Girls: Supports and Challenges

GIRLS	SCHOOL	ONE STRATEGY USED	WHAT HELPED	SOME CHALLENGES
Keisha	Garth Urban East Coast	Speaking out: Maverick leader	Principal asked her to join leadership committee Classroom aide and community member as mentors Parents behind her Own determination	Tendency to confront adults can be problematic Transition to high school means leaving mentors Societal class/race prejudice
Mona	Avila Rural Southwest	Speaking out: Troublemaker	Programs that develop creativity Family belief in her talents Ability to express herself Involvement in this research	Mulitple cultural spheres to negotiate Adult perceptions of her as "negative leader" Societal class/race prejudice Gang culture
Hillary	Fairfield Rural South	Doing school: Schoolgirl	Teachers' affirmation Congruence of home and school values Own diligence and kindness	Overcoming conventional expectations Developmental changes Peer pressures
Josephine	Valley Stream Suburban West Coast	Doing school: Play schoolgirl	School counselor as mentor Involvement in peer mediation program Leadership opportunities at school Own self-awareness	Recent move to neighborhood Pressures to conform
Angela	Parkside Urban East Coast	Crossing Borders: Schoolgirl/cool girl	Mother's involvement with school Small learning community with invested core teacher Teaching approaches that offer a range of roles	Racial/ethnic prejudices Own ambivalence about leadership Mother's involvement with school
Nikki	Madison Suburban Midwest	Crossing borders: Translator	School policies that emphasize commitment to equity Mother as mentor Administrative recognition Leadership role in school Own self-reflectiveness	Perception by some that she's a "bully" Societal racial/ethnic prejudices Own ambivalence about translator role

Hillary began the year new to Fairfield, a rural middle school in the South. Over the summer, her family moved here from a smaller and more isolated rural community so her dad could take a job at Fairfield Industries and to be closer to Hillary's grandmother. Hillary's mother now commutes thirty minutes to her part-time job as manager in a doctor's office. Hillary is glad to be in Fairfield where she is able to spend more time with her grandmother, who lives in a trailer five minutes from Hillary's house. Closely connected to an extended family of aunts, uncles, and cousins, Hillary recounts stories of overnights with her grandmother who cooks her favorite foods and inscribed the "names of all of her grandchildren—even the baby who died—in the sidewalk outside her trailer"; weekly dinners with cousins who accompany her to a church study group; a family vacation to Florida that was "special and great" despite "a trashy motel that had a leaky roof and still cost a fortune to stay in."

Here at her new school, adults and students alike took quickly to Hillary. When she was hospitalized in the fall with a virus that caused severe vertigo, Hillary received what a teacher called "an outpouring of concern and affection. I'll never forget one little boy—one of our sweeter but slower students—wrote Hillary: 'You're my best friend. You are always nice to everybody.'" Hillary displays this "nice" quality by helping a girl with fewer resources than she has:

> Gym: A test on tennis is scheduled for this period. Hillary sits on the bleachers going over her notes and complaining with a friend that scoring is "so complicated." Dawn, a heavy girl who had been sitting alone, approaches Hillary and asks if she can look at her notes because she has been absent. Hillary suggests that Dawn talk to the teacher about not taking the test. When Hillary sees that Dawn is unsuccessful with the gym teacher, she gives her notes to her.
>
> (From a researcher's fieldnotes, 2/1/95)

Frequently dressed in corduroys and plaid shirts neatly tucked into belted pants, Hillary has the "prep" look that Fairfield students contrast to "redneck" or sometimes "good ole country." She likes country music but "doesn't mind listening to gospel with my mom in the car. But I wouldn't tell her that I like it." One teacher perceives Hillary as "natural and less sophisticated than some of our students." When asked about leaders in her class, Hillary—like many of her peers—quickly names Megan and Angie because "everybody knows them and likes them. They're cheerleaders." Then, more thoughtfully, she adds one of the first girls to befriend her, someone unnamed by anyone else: "Elizabeth is good in school. She does all her work. She tells her opinion. She speaks up for herself."

During the course of the research, Hillary exhibits changes familiar to observers of middle school youngsters. In November one of her friends explains that when she first moved to Fairfield, all the boys, especially Kurt, wanted to be Hillary's boyfriend but "she wouldn't have any of them." Hillary retorts, "I don't want a boyfriend. Boys are annoying." In January Hillary identifies Kurt as a class leader and even expresses some admiration for him: "Kurt is a live one. He picks on people and plays with them and does well in school.... Him and Chevez won the story award." By March a teacher-researcher writes that Hillary and Kurt are now "going together" and that the science teacher had to speak to them about "sneaking a kiss" during class. She reports that she has spoken to Hillary's mother: "Issues with peer pressure are coming up for Hillary now. She is maturing physically and her mother is nervous about it."

Hillary's behavior in science class is interpreted in light of her image as a "schoolgirl." She's not bad, her teacher concludes, just "maturing physically" and responding to "peer pressure." Her new behaviors over the year alert us to the developmental dimension of girls' strategies. For example, as they begin seventh grade, girls may be more likely to employ a seamless schoolgirl strategy as Hillary does; as they move toward eighth grade, they must learn to balance school demands with changing social expectations.

Asked about her future, Hillary echoes the hopes and concerns that many Fairfield residents hold for area girls and young women:

> I want to be a teacher or a radiologist. If I am a teacher I want first- or seventh-grade kids. When I was at my old school I helped out with the first graders. I loved it. I really got attached to those kids and was so sorry to leave them. Those kids still remember me when I see them at church. I would like seventh grade because it would be a challenge. If I was a radiologist I would go to Clayton Hospital. They have a two-year program there. I don't know if I'll have the money to go to college.

A Play Schoolgirl. Hundreds of miles away in a different school setting, a girl exhibits another dimension of the "doing school" strategy. Like Hillary, Josephine "does school" well, meeting traditional school expectations. Unlike Hillary, though, Josephine recounts considerable struggle in her effort to fit in and negotiate her eighth-grade niche at her academic award-winning, suburban West Coast middle school. A high-achieving youngster, she keeps her uncertainty, her pain, and perhaps much of her creativity under wraps.

Josephine is a tall, slender, blond Caucasian with delicate features and high cheekbones. The jeans and plaid oversized workshirt with sturdy sandals suit the angularity of her body and mark her as knowing what is "in" at her school. Her name is mentioned by several Valley Stream girls as their "ideal," and their comments carry a wishful chorus of "if I could be like Josephine...." When we discuss whether girls here can be both "successful with teachers" and "popular," her name comes up. Josephine also takes her role as the lead eighth-grade peer mediator very seriously.

Only after a researcher has gained her trust and pressed her to speak does she volunteer, "I moved here a year ago, which was really hard for me. I think I've changed a lot since that move. I've become a really different person." She reflects on how sports are "a real priority" in this school and town, and sees herself as "a terrible athlete," more of an artist. She contrasts this setting with the urban school three hours south that she attended previously: "Where I came from, it wasn't a very good part of town and they had a lot of outreach to the students. They had all these clubs, drama, psychology, and all these exciting things to do." When her mother remarried and relocated here, it was the beginning of a "hard, dark time" for Josephine. "It was pretty bad for a while, but all of a sudden, when you go through pain that's that intense you start to come out on the other side."

An adult at school, a female counselor, stepped in and made the difference, Josephine readily acknowledges:

> She is definitely a role model for me. It's easy to talk to people who are a lot like you. And I think we have a lot in common. She kind of understood what I was going through and how it was hard for me to adjust and everything. She took extra time to help me out, listened to me, understood that I was in real pain. A lot of people they said, "Okay, you'll get over it." And of course I did get over it. But it was nice to have somebody there who said, "No, what you're feeling is definitely valid and real."

The counselor identified peer mediation as a program in which Josephine could find her voice. Josephine trained to become a mediator. She credits her success in this program to her struggle to adjust: "When you have experienced pain, you then understand others' pain better." When asked about her strengths, she replies, "I feel like I can understand people really well. I have a real kinship with almost everyone I know. I'm really close to people."

Josephine has a good male friend who helps her put in perspective her need to conform to others' expectations. "He thinks it's hilarious that I worry about all these people and then think that I am not a good person unless I make everyone happy."

In addition to being lead peer mediator with major responsibilities for training the "interns" in the seventh grade, Josephine is treasurer of the Student Government Association, a hands-on position that requires her to respond to weekly requests for activity funds from both staff and students. She takes honors classes and is in the top algebra class. She laments,

> I get A's and B's but I really want straight A's. I feel that I could be doing better but it's really hard when you have all kinds of other things that people want you to do. People are always saying, "Okay, you have to do this and this and this, and you only have this much time to do it."

Josephine values her relationships with adults at school and accepts responsibilities they place on her even when their expectations are "unreasonable."

Josephine has a good male friend—not a boyfriend, she's careful to say; she doesn't want one yet, though boys ask her out—who helps her put in perspective her need to conform to others' expectations. "We talk about stuff and he thinks it's hilarious that I worry about all these people and then think that I am not a good person unless I make everyone happy." Friendship, respect, and admiration mean a great deal to Josephine because "when I was younger, I was real skinny. I had kind of short hair and didn't wear nice clothes. I used to go out on the field and sit by myself and just sing to myself."

Now an aspiring opera singer, Josephine takes weekly voice lessons. "When I was real young, I knew that I wanted to sing. I wanted my voice to be beautiful. My parents tell stories where I would go around the house saying, 'Turn on the lady' [Julie Andrews singing *The Sound of Music*]." Her mother celebrates her daughter's talents but also recognizes her struggle not to be subsumed by others' expectations.

Reflecting on Girls Who Do School. While both Hillary and Josephine provide examples of girls "doing school" in conventionally approved ways, they also demonstrate subtly divergent strategies. Their approaches reflect differences in their schools' cultures as well as in the girls' identities and choices.

New arrivals to their respective schools, Hillary and Josephine were named by their teachers only months into the school year as successful girls. Both take their roles as students seriously, completing all that is required of them, appreciating adults who take time with them, and meeting peers' as well as adults' expectations. Both take pride in their work and their grades. Both are white in predominantly white settings, though Hillary's is a rural Southern school while Josephine's is suburban and on the West Coast. But the two girls employ somewhat divergent strategies for success. While Hillary seems to fit easily into her new life and school culture, "doing school" without apparent effort, Josephine struggles to manage conflicting expectations as she both conforms to a schoolgirl role and seeks to know and be herself. The greater degree of pressure at her school ups the ante for Josephine in her effort to find a balance between others' needs and her own.

Hillary employs negotiating strategies that match traditional expectations for girls in this setting. Women in the school who grew up in the area can recognize in Hillary the same values with which they were raised, the same roles they assumed, and the same achievements and limitations reached. While at several points Hillary betrays her awareness that her family's modest means may limit her goals, nevertheless she seems confident that her abilities and her persona will pave future options.

Josephine boasts a strong school record, too. But in conversation she articulates a more complex picture involving pain and struggle. Although she evidences considerable skill at "playing school"—both academically and socially—Josephine is aware that she is indeed playing multiple roles expected by adults as well as peers in her life. By talking with her male friend about her conflict over her multiple roles, Josephine demonstrates a successful if private way to pursue inquiry into gender issues. At the same time,

Josephine's ability to call up her own struggle as a way of connecting with others' challenges is a strength that lets her be more empathetic. It remains to be seen if her sense of her own emerging identity will balance the pressures to conform to others' expectations and meet others' needs as she moves on to high school.

For Hillary and Josephine, school presents a site for success, and school adults acknowledge and support their achievements. But looking at the ways in which these two girls "do school" also suggests the need for reforms that would help schools expand girls' possibilities. Both girls would benefit from the opportunity to try out a range of roles and personae in school without risking safety and acceptance. For Hillary, a structured opportunity to step into a leadership role might broaden her repertoire of strategies. For Josephine, fewer adult demands on her time and more opportunities to explore her own creativity might help her balance her emerging identity with her position as a school leader.

Crossing Borders

A Schoolgirl/Cool Girl. Angela presents herself as the epitome of what many middle school girls might aspire to become—well groomed, stylishly attired, attractive, poised, confident, popular, and excelling academically. A thirteen-year-old Puerto Rican girl, she attends a community middle school in an ethnically and racially diverse, working-class neighborhood in one of the major cities in the Northeast corridor.

Being physically attractive is not always an attribute that lends itself to popularity with both girls and boys in middle school. Nevertheless, Angela has developed a facility with her peers—relating adeptly with girls as well as boys while also preserving her sense of self. As a result of this ability, she is viewed as a leader in her advisory section, in her classes, and in the larger school culture.

Voted president of her advisory, Angela has a leadership style that mixes quiet reserve and steadfast determination. She has learned how to survive and flourish in a school culture where the values of adults who hold structural power are often at odds with the adolescent value system in which students must negotiate. Angela has figured out the behaviors adults hold in high regard. And she has discovered that behaviors that boys find acceptable—such as being outspoken, even argumentative at times, and not following the rules—differ from behaviors teachers expect from girls. Savvy about this tension, Angela manages on occasion to exhibit male-approved behaviors without rebuke, perhaps because her teachers are perplexed at this atypical stance.

Angela steps in and out of both the adult value system and her peer culture, which includes pressure and intimidation from boys, thus maintaining her integrity as a bright, able young woman. In the following vignette, Angela interacts with a male classmate and their science teacher, Joel Levy, keeping her self-respect and independence by not allowing males to dominate her intellectually or socially:

> Since Soeun, Gloria, and Angela missed their science period with Mr. Levy this morning, he used Advisory to give the girls their topics for their reports on constellations. When Angela was given Sevis, the whale, one of the boys snidely called her a whale. Angela stated in a steady, deliberate tone, "I am not a whale." The teacher, unaware of the boy's comment, offered, "You are doing a report on the whale constellation." Assuredly and in a tone bordering on arrogance, Angela retorted, "Yes, I know!" Mr. Levy, looking perplexed by her tenor, made no counter response.
>
> (From a researcher's fieldnotes, 10/12/94)

In this scenario, Angela demonstrates her capability and willingness not to "let things go." She steps out of her schoolgirl role. She could have opted to remain silent— first with the boy and then with the teacher—but instead makes a concerted and deliberate effort to have her voice heard. This behavior is somewhat inconsistent with her general demeanor, which is to court some degree of invisibility: Not standing out gives her favorable stature in both the adult and peer cultures in the school. Although Angela is rarely observed participating openly in class discussions, her teachers applaud her as an excellent student.

Angela also is able to identify male privilege and turn it to her own advantage. In this vignette, Angela tries out the conventional strategy of hand-raising before arriving at the more successful strategy of enlisting the aid of a male peer:

> The two eighth-grade classes were facing each other across a playing field. Camaraderie was fostered by the game's design and scoring system. Students screamed and supported classmates passionately. Angela stood on the sidelines, very much in control. Her long chestnut hair was pulled back in a ponytail that exposed gold hoop earrings, and she was stylishly attired in ivory jeans and a maize sweater. When teams were being switched, she raised her hand but was not selected. Angela gestured to a classmate, a large boy who had scored a number of goals. The noise in the gym was deafening, but she gestured to explain that she had not had a chance to play. The boy interrupted the gym teacher, risking losing points, to intercede. As a result, a girl left the original line-up and Angela went in.
>
> (From a researcher's fieldnotes, 10/12/94)

Referred to often as a leader, Angela demonstrates her individualism by controlling the degree to which she will allow adults to coerce her. Urged on by teachers to run for president of the student body, she resists. When asked about student council, she expresses disdain for the way boys make rude remarks about the girls' physical appearance in assembly: "I don't want to be bothered with all of that." Her rejection of the formal leadership role reminds us of how important it is to look with girls' eyes: While adults tend to view student council as an ideal "voice" mechanism in school, Angela is more concerned with the negative trappings of the position than with its possible advantages.

Angela's decision not to participate formally in school leadership is also interesting in light of the fact that her stepmother is president of the Home and School Association, the local equivalent of the Parent Teacher Association. An articulate and outspoken woman, the stepmother is more than willing to raise difficult issues for discussion by the school's administrators and teachers. Informed of a policy recently initiated in the lunchroom, Angela's stepmother reflects, "I didn't know about it because my daughter didn't tell me. She tells me some things but not everything because she doesn't want me to go into the office and talk about it." Being the middle school daughter of a high-profile mother may contribute to Angela's desire to maintain a low school profile.

In Angela's interactions with adults, she is not overly friendly and does not attempt to ingratiate herself. Her manner is cool and somewhat detached. In this way, she protects her privacy, increases her capital with her teachers who have certain expectations of female students, and simultaneously fits comfortably into her peer culture.

A Translator. In the Midwest, a girl of similar talents but without Angela's studied aloofness seeks to maintain her independence even as she mediates for others across disparate cultures in her school community. A tall, fully developed African American girl with a loud voice, Nikki has been identified by administrators, teachers, and peers as a "natural leader" in her mostly white, suburban middle school. Apparently able to code-switch at will, Nikki communicates and holds sway with adults and teens across lines of race and class. She acts as an ally to an administration striving for a safe and orderly environment as well as to students—perhaps particularly female and African American students—who appreciate the authority she bears. In fact, her word carries so much authority that at times she is perceived by some adults and students as wielding too much power in the school. Both her assertiveness and her cooperation with school authorities flout the rules of a peer culture that typically rewards invisibility and moderate insubordination.

Nikki herself is less interested in securing others' approval than in pursuing her own sense of right thinking and action. She exhibits the ability to stand firmly for what she believes; peer pressure seems to have less impact on her conscious decisions than it does for many young people. Nikki describes herself this way: "See, I have a very strong mind that you would have to persuade if you wanted me to do something. Like if you wanted me to try drugs or whatever, I would think about all the perspectives and everything." This demonstrably stable sense of self seems also surprisingly receptive, an identity being shaped over time by a reflective sensibility.

Although she values her own company, Nikki is not a loner. An appreciation of mutual respect seems to drive her relationships with peers as well as adults. A friend describes Nikki as "a leader to me because she gives 100 percent. I give her my 100 percent respect because she gives it to me. And a lot of other people give her their respect. So I look up to Nikki. I'm not going to say she's a role model but...."

Nikki acts with restraint in a class where she sees the male teacher as sexist and racist, so as not to hurt her grade. But she tempers that restraint when he confronts her in the halls: "Outside class...I'm gonna give him respect, because that's what my mom taught me, but I'm not gonna give him 100 percent."

For Nikki, respect is central, though it may look different in different spheres of her life: "I know with my mother, I show my mother a little more respect than I show my friends. I respect my friends but in a different manner. With the teacher, I'm not two-faced or whatever. I just show more respect. That's how I was raised."

Nikki's life has not been a simple linear tale of achievement. Sexually abused by a neighbor when she was a young girl, she knew how to support a friend who was sexually assaulted. The abuse provided a harsh lesson and strengthened her resolve "not to let people walk all over me." Incidents of racism have also pressed her to call her own assertiveness into service. How has she used these challenges to gain an understanding of others' perspectives and not instead to justify anger, hatred, and blame? She answers the question this way: "I have a conscience and I have a heart."

Nikki reflects habitually on her own behavior, subjecting past actions to new scrutiny as her ideas mature. For example, she recalls that last year she sometimes felt she was "being treated differently in a class because I was black." Later she considered the possibility that "that wasn't the case...I realized I have to think from both sides." This year she sifts through others' sometimes contradictory expectations of her: "Boys, mom, the adults, they want me to do this thing, and my friends want me to come over here and do this, but you have to compromise. I'll be like, 'I'll do half of this and then I'll go and do this.'...It's about learning this year."

Adults in school demonstrate their high expectations of Nikki by placing her in leadership roles that require her to cross borders such as age and race to translate for people on either side. A peer mediator, Nikki is expected to use her mediating skills not only in occasional formal sessions but also daily in hallways and other public spaces to help students and minimize school disruptions. Nikki both internalizes and resents these expectations: "I get treated more strict than anybody in this school. Because I'm a big talker, I'm supposed to show an example." She describes an instance where her role seems impossible: "I'm trying to stop some playing around [in the hallway] and all these teachers start yelling at me and I'm trying to stop trouble for them!...All my friends are like, they get to have fun."

A friend describes how Nikki took on the usually adult role of disciplinarian at the basketball game the previous day:

> Before [the adults] could say, "Stop stepping on the bleachers," you could hear Nikki saying, "Stop stepping on the bleachers."...She was cheering for all teams.

She don't take that. That's the good thing about her. If you have a fight she won't take sides. She'll say, "Why'd you all do this? Why don't you talk it out?"

The school's harnessing of Nikki's mediating abilities can also spell trouble for a strong, reflective girl who takes that charge seriously, as in the following incident:

> Before Christmas, Nikki was suspended in coming to the rescue of a student involved in an altercation with a girl "from the city." Nikki intervened, telling the girl, "That's not how we do things here. We don't fight." The city girl informed her that she would "kick her ass too" and the fight ensued. For this infraction, Nikki served a one day in-house suspension with her mom present, shadowing her daughter all day. Note that this is an option—either three days out of school or one day in school with a parent.
> (From a researcher's fieldnotes, 1/27/95)

Nikki's mother is a reliable, competent, and caring advocate for her daughter. In fact, Nikki names her mother and poet Maya Angelou as the two women she admires most: "[My mother] talks to me and respects me. She talks to me like I'm not just her daughter [but] her friend, her sister, whatever. I just like the whole style about my mother." And about Maya Angelou: "As soon as I read her book [*I Know Why the Caged Bird Sings*, 1969], I knew I wanted to be just like her. How she went places and made a difference, how she overcame the odds.... Like I don't want to be the president of the United States, but it would be nice."

While Nikki has internalized adult expectations that promote success, almost parroting her math teacher's caution that in high school "they expect so much more," she also uses her skills as a translator of others' cultures to figure out what's needed to succeed without forfeiting more of herself than she's willing to lose. She acts with restraint in a class where she sees the male teacher as sexist and racist, so as not to hurt her grade. But she tempers that restraint when he confronts her in the halls: "I'm gonna participate in class but if we're outside school or outside class... I'm gonna give him respect, because that's what my mom taught me, but I'm not gonna give him 100 percent."

Nikki's grades and national test scores are generally high, and she has high hopes for the future:

> I want to be a lawyer....I know I'm gonna try, and I know I'm gonna succeed, but if I can't do that, I'll resort to like a juvenile worker, helper, assistant. I want to give back to the community what they gave to me. I just want to make a difference, because they say you can make a difference.

Reflecting on Girls Who Cross Borders. Angela and Nikki are recognized by adults and peers for their ability to cross borders, decipher complex messages, and respond appropriately in the several different cultures of school and community. Nikki describes herself as "tolerant" of a range of people and situations. Angela also demonstrates forbearance in the many situations that she observes without entering the fray. This ability to understand diverse perspectives seems to indicate a strong sense of self—or at least confidence in the process of coming into self—rather than the chameleon lack of self for which this ability is often mistaken.

Both young women are also experiencing considerable pressure from school adults to employ their talents in the service of the school. In both cases the pressure comes from female administrators committed to school reforms that include an awareness of gender issues.

Angela resists the pressure to use her skills as a border crosser in an official and ongoing way. Thus she evades a formal role while retaining the ability to step in when she chooses in support of a teacher, a girl or boy friend, or herself. Nikki, on the other hand, protests her assigned role as school leader and the expectation that she translate across cultures for the good of the school, but in fact accedes to these expectations. While peer mediation gives her a chance to use her strengths publicly, she is also burdened by the expectation that she, as mediator, identify with the institution rather than with her peers. This tension peaks when Nikki confronts an African American young woman "from the city" who is not yet acculturated to the school. While Nikki's strengths have been channeled into leadership at Madison, in this instance she confronts a girl whose strengths have developed differently; for Nikki, this young woman may provide a troubling reflection.

Young women who carry tremendous expectations from adults as well as peers, Angela and Nikki use a shared set of strategies but make different choices. As these girls are pressed to employ their considerable strengths in many arenas simultaneously, their stories compel us to ask how schools might help them to keep this balancing act from overwhelming them. When adults in schools make a conscious effort to acknowledge differences, raising questions of gender, age, race, and culture, for example, in discussions of classroom dynamics and in the curriculum, they transfer the job of understanding others from the shoulders of a few "border crossers" to the community as a whole.

Implications

Adolescent girls typically undertake the process of identity-making with conscious effort, pain, uncertainty, and creativity. As active agents choosing and revising their approaches, girls are engaged in a continuous cycle of action and reaction with their environments. Since school takes up a disproportionately large part of their lives, it is not surprising that a great deal of this identity work goes on in school.

Because all young adolescent girls—even those achieving marked conventional successes—are engaged in this developmental process, their emergent selves are likely to be new, fragile, vulnerable to assault. What works for one girl at one school may not work for another girl at another school or even for the same girl from one year to the next. Girls who speak out may be treated as leaders or renegades. Girls who "do school" may be seen as "good" or may be invisible to adults. Girls who cross borders may be perceived as talented or power-hungry. Thus Josephine, acclaimed in her Valley Stream school setting, continues to struggle with insecurities prompted by her family's relocation. Between the researchers' visits to Avila in the rural Southwest, Mona changes, at least in her teachers' estimation, from a "leader" to a "troublemaker." Schoolgirl Hillary "sneaks a kiss" with her first boyfriend. Eighth graders describe their journey through middle school: Many begin as "schoolgirls" but find peer expectations increasingly pitted against those of the school culture. Clearly, no single negotiating approach will benefit all girls in all settings. Shifting strategies may help girls cope.

School adults need to notice the different ways that girls negotiate school. This requires observing girls in hallways and classrooms, asking girls questions, attending to girls' voices. It is also important that adults understand girls' needs to try out strategies in the process of forming identities and recognize that girls' strategies may shift. When adults become aware of how the culture of their schools and classrooms helps to shape girls' strategies, then they can help girls understand and increase their options and make conscious strategic decisions.

In this chapter we have looked at how six girls are negotiating their school lives. Each of these girls adopts strategies and tries on identities in ways characteristic of many of the girls we met in this study. These girls' successes testify to the support of adults in their lives and to their schools' efforts to incorporate what we're learning about adolescent development and gender as well as to their own hard work. While we began this study by looking for a relatively linear connection between what schools are doing and how their successful girls are faring, what we found instead was that successful girls and their schools are engaged in a complex, dynamic relationship that is neither linear nor necessarily cumulative. What works for girls involves a repertoire of possibilities.

These cases help illustrate the complexity of all factors working on girls. Gender and the way society interprets gender are not the only factors influencing a girl in middle school, but they are critical factors. The cases also highlight the opportunity for schools—if they're aware of these factors—to tailor curricula and programs to match girls' needs. In Chapter Three we go inside three schools—a suburban, an urban, and a rural middle school—to investigate their approaches to middle school reform and gender equity. We view what is going on in these schools from the perspectives of both girls and adults, highlighting both what schools do that affects girls' opportunities, and how girls interpret and respond to their options for school success.

CHAPTER THREE

SCHOOL SNAPSHOTS:
DIFFERING VIEWS OF GENDER

In the last chapter we mapped girls' general approaches to negotiating school, showing girls as agents weighing options and trying out strategies in a process of identity formation. Now we examine more closely the contexts in which they do so. Because girls spend so much time in school, much of their identity work goes on there.

In Chapter Three we look inside three middle schools—a suburban, urban, and rural school. From the sometimes differing perspectives of school adults and successful girls, we examine how the schools support their girls and where they fall short. Looking at what works for girls in school carries implications for adolescent boys as well. Middle school reforms that are good for girls tend to expand the options of all students and provide forums for examining their experiences; such reforms also have beneficial consequences for adolescent boys, who confront a distinct but analogous set of developmental issues.

In this chapter we take school "snapshots," freezing particular moments in the dynamic lives of the schools. We enter hallways, classrooms, and gymnasiums, stopping the action to invite students and adults to reflect on gender issues. Our snapshots look across the "five Ps" of people, places, programs, priorities, and policies that the AAUW Educational Foundation's research has identified as salient dimensions of schools.[28] As we observed and listened, these patterns of difference emerged:

- Suburban schools tended to define gender issues in terms of challenges to be met through policy and program initiatives. For example, these schools implemented sexual harassment policies, a math program that addressed girls' needs, and a teacher development program that focused on gender issues. Girls in suburban schools were able to point to policies and programs that addressed gender equity both explicitly and implicitly.

- Urban schools tended to define gender issues in the context of the many challenges facing low-income, minority youngsters—both male and female. Adults, particularly women, made a priority of their connections with girls, often acknowledging their own challenges as they offered girls academic, social, and emotional support.[29] Girls in urban schools readily named school-based and community adults who took time and energy to mentor and advocate for them.
- Rural schools tended to approach gender issues indirectly. In defining success for their girls, these school communities struggled to uphold traditional gender assumptions while they prepared girls for a changing world. Without addressing gender per se, these schools instituted middle school reforms that encouraged girls to develop such qualities as competence and independence. For example, the rural schools had strong, respected athletic programs for girls. Girls in rural schools speak of places in school where they are taken seriously—praised as well as challenged.

In the pages that follow, we take a close-up look at a Midwestern suburban school, an East Coast urban school, and a Southwestern rural school. These schools provide an opportunity to highlight different approaches to gender:

- In the Midwestern suburban school, we focus on the sexual harassment policy recently put into place. In a school where gender equity is supported explicitly in policy and programs, we ask, how do students and adults experience school climate in classrooms, hallways, the gymnasium?
- In the East Coast urban school, adults describe challenges shared by low-income African American and Latino girls and boys as well as issues that divide. Aided by a middle school reform that groups staff and students into smaller learning communities or "houses," adults and girls forge connections; our snapshot focuses on these. In a setting where adolescents are facing harsh social inequities, we ask, how do adults and girls experience challenges and supports?
- In the Southwestern rural school, we meet youngsters dealing with mounting economic and social pressures in traditional communities with a dwindling employment base. In the context of the school's efforts to boost student achievement by implementing reforms such as collaborative learning and career exploration, we focus on how girls and adults experience those practices that support and those that hinder girls' success.

School Snapshot

Name: Madison Junior High

Where: Suburban Midwest

Size: Approximately 800 students

Class makeup: 80% white, 10% African American, some Asian and Latino

Tall, slender, and blond, Melissa enters the two-story brick building along with other early arrivals. Moving down the seventh-grade corridor, she passes sienna lockers lining the Star Team hallway—adorned with its galaxy of yellow stars with student names—to arrive at her locker in the Pride Team hall. The Pride Team includes the only remaining "gifted" sections in an otherwise detracked system. Book bag in hand, Melissa turns into a carpeted room where a few others sit at rows of desks under soundproofed ceiling tiles. This is her advisory class—what used to be known as homeroom.

At the bell Melissa navigates the hallway to first period, a predominantly white class with roughly equal numbers of boys and girls. The science teacher passes around jars containing samples: star worms, millipedes, a fetal pig. Students are determining phylum and similarities. They treat the samples clinically, examining them closely, reading pertinent information, and passing them forward to the next person. When a jar reaches Melissa, she tries to pass it to the boy in front of her. He sits sideways, arm flung across her desk, looking at the jar but not taking it. She returns the sample jar to the table. This scene recurs. After she examines a jellyfish, smiling at what she sees, then passing it on with success this time, Melissa points for the boy to return this third specimen. He resists, grumbling, "Always making me do stuff," before complying. Then he grabs her book. She lunges forward, takes it out of his hands, and slaps it down loudly. Unaware of this interaction, the teacher leads a lively lesson on classification in the animal kingdom. At each question, twenty or so hands fly up. A girl raises several questions. Boys consistently raise questions and insert comments.

Labeled a gifted student, Melissa employs a schoolgirl strategy, completing all work and doing as asked in class. When she has trouble with an assignment, "I find out what I did, I relax about it, and I try to correct my problems." Her science teacher describes her as "very personable, helps out, conscientious, and self-confident." But the teacher doesn't seem to recognize that Melissa has a problem: Melissa asked a researcher to attend her science class because she was disturbed by the boy in front of her. Melissa's teacher, occupied with the lesson and sure of Melissa's "conscientiousness," meanwhile remains oblivious to the daily provocations that distract Melissa from science—in spite of a schoolwide policy on harassment and staff development on equity in the classroom.

Melissa's situation illustrates the unevenness of change in a setting where gender equity is named as a priority. A boy's circular reasoning during a focus group reveals his struggle to make sense of shifting roles:

> Boy: A long time ago or whatever…like the girl would stay home and stuff and the guys would go out and work. And it's like changing because everything's like equal now. And I guess it would be okay if a girl tried out for wrestling because if she wanted to do something, I mean, I'd let her do whatever she wanted to do as long as it's okay.
> Researcher: What makes it okay or not?
> Boy: Well, if a guy can do it, I guess a girl can do it.

Like the scene in Melissa's classroom, the boy's comments point up the limits of a school's push for gender equity. A harassment policy doesn't guarantee change in every setting. A boy sees that "everything's like equal now" but still views girls' options in light of boys' activities.

Gender in a Suburban School: Girls' and Adults' Perspectives. Situated in a predominantly white, middle-class district where top-level administrators are addressing equity issues, Madison has begun to make gender equity visible at the level of policy. The school is located in a suburban village of 25,000 surrounded by miles of strip malls and tract housing, and twenty-five miles from a large Midwestern city. A relatively remote bedroom community a decade ago, the area has recently had an influx of city dwellers and now includes fourteen units of subsidized housing. African American students from the city tend to be poorer than those here longer, while the Asian Americans tend to be middle class. Latinos are the newest immigrants, a language minority group. In this increasingly diverse setting, Madison teachers participate in a districtwide training program called GESA (Gender/Ethnic Expectations and Student Achievement), designed to help teachers make student classrooms equitable. (GESA is described more fully in Chapter Four.)

The sexual harassment policy was drafted during the 1993-94 school year after a district administrator signed the principal up for an AAUW workshop called "Hostile Hallways." Hired several years ago, the principal followed three male predecessors, each of whom during his tenure headed a school with a reputation for resisting change. Although she felt the workshop's name did not describe her school, the principal found that the session "opened my eyes and ears" to the many subtle and less subtle forms of harassment that take place daily at school. She asked staff, parents, and students to help draft a policy. They did. An excerpt reads:

> Sexual harassment of students is prohibited. Sexual harassment is defined as…unwelcome sexual advances, requests for sexual favors, and other verbal or physical conduct of a sexual or sex-based nature by anyone, including students, that have the purpose or effect of (a) substantially interfering with a student's

educational environment; (b) creating an intimidating, hostile, or offensive educational environment; (c) or depriving a student of educational aid, benefits, services or treatment.

(Madison Student/Parent Handbook)

The policy is just one evidence of a school climate that boasts physical as well as financial security. The school hallways, offices, library, and lunchroom look relatively new and well cared for. Classrooms are equipped with both chalk and marker boards. Books, supplies, and audiovisual and lab equipment are plentiful and well maintained. Outside are ample playing fields, with up-to-date athletic equipment stored in a spacious gymnasium. The school has adopted, and students generally adhere to, a strict discipline code. Classes begin promptly. Unexcused absences result in detention or suspension. And note-passing—prohibited even in hallways—is grounds for a search, intended as part of a larger campaign to deter gang activity. Classrooms, with their seats usually arranged in rows, tend to follow traditional formats, such as a lecture followed by a question-and-answer period and individual work.

The school's sexual harassment policy is now in its first year. Seventh-grade girls describe it as part of a culture of constraint that both protects and thwarts them:

> I think [the policy] is good.

> Yeah. But they take it too seriously. Someone can go like this to someone [putting an arm around friend's shoulder] and if the teacher sees you, it's like, oh, that's sexual harassment.

> My brother's going out with somebody and he put his arm around her and he got in trouble. They said he was touching her in a bad way. It was just like putting his arm around her.

> I think that's wrong because in seventh grade you're supposed to have more freedom and more opportunities with boys and stuff.

A Student-Teacher Dialogue on Sexual Harassment. Teacher-researchers participating in *Girls in the Middle* wanted to learn more about how their students perceived the harassment policy. They invited female and male students to participate for several weeks in a dialogue journal—a written exchange of thoughts, concerns, and questions between student and teacher. These journals gave students a structured opportunity to think about their concepts of sexually appropriate and inappropriate behavior. Participation was voluntary. Although the exercise didn't work equally well for all participants, excerpts show how the dialogue journal gave Glinnie—a thoughtful seventh grader—a chance to articulate her ideas and incorporate new dimensions suggested by her teacher, Joann Gordon:

Dear Glinnie,
Thanks for agreeing to dialogue with me about such a sensitive issue! I think it's probably necessary to start by defining sexual harassment since that is our focus. I'd also like for you to think about these questions: Do you feel that boys and girls are treated equally in our school? Have you ever seen a case that may be construed as sexual harassment? How would you define sexual harassment? Thanks!

Mrs. Gordon

Boys and girls get treated differently but not all the time. In P.E. it sometimes seems like they try and make the boys work harder. No, I haven't seen any situation that would be considered sexual harassment. Like popping bras, I don't really consider it sexual harassment but more of a friendly or playing type. I would define sexual harassment as feeling or touching someone in a way they wouldn't like.

Glinnie

Dear Glinnie,
Your definition of sexual harassment is interesting. You believe that it is limited to unwanted sexual advances. Can the definition also be extended to include name-calling, looks, or body language?

Mrs. Gordon

Yes, the definition can include name-calling, looks, or body language. But again it depends on the age and the people. I think for junior high students some kids might consider name-calling, looks, or body language flattering. Again it depends on the person. If a boy keeps looking at you, most young girls think, he likes me.

Glinnie

Dear Glinnie,
So your definition has changed and broadened. What's your new definition? I think it is very interesting to note that sexual harassment depends on the age and the person. But how can we generalize the definition to include everyone? Or can we? Do you know about our school's sexual harassment policy? Do you think victims would take advantage of the policy and the services it offers? Have you ever seen any cases that somebody else could construe as sexual harassment?

Mrs. Gordon

If a woman or anyone doesn't want to do what you want them to do, then that's sexual harassment. I know a little bit about the sexual harassment system. I know that if someone is touching someone in a place where they don't want to be touched, then they might get a detention, a Saturday detention, or a suspension, depending on how bad it is. I don't really think that anyone would take advantage of the system because most people don't want to feel uncomfortable. No, I haven't seen any case that someone else could consider sexual harassment. Well it was a long time ago, but a girl told me and some other people that at the school dance some boy came up to her and was touching her. I didn't see it.

Glinnie

Dear Glinnie,
We do have a sexual harassment policy in place that is much more involved than simply issuing detentions. Do you have any suggestions as to how we can spread the word to students about the policy? Did the girl at the dance do anything about the incident?

Mrs. Gordon

> I think there could be an assembly or some kind of gathering with students and that would help the students further know about the sexual harassment policy. I don't think the girl did anything about the incident. She just told her friends that some boy was touching over her.
>
> Glinnie

Glinnie's definition of sexual harassment as limited to unwanted sexual attention is distinctly different from the broad and multifaceted one outlined by the policy. For her, there is a large and exciting realm of good, explicitly sexual interaction between girls and boys. Telling good sex from bad is not difficult: If you like the attention, it's good; if not, it's bad. As Glinnie and others indicate, good sexual interactions can include behaviors such as bra snapping and hugging that are not sanctioned by school policy.

Glinnie and Mrs. Gordon both learn from each other and retain core viewpoints: While Glinnie's definition of sexual harassment changes somewhat, expanding to include name-calling, for example, she retains the distinction between good and bad sexual attention. Mrs. Gordon seems genuinely interested in Glinnie's thoughts but also carries the agenda of figuring out an effective way to disseminate information on the policy. She walks a fine line as both listener and institutional agent.

A Need for Other Initiatives. Girls as well as teachers identify gaps in the policy and its implementation. Eighth-grade girls feel betrayed by the school's apparent inability to protect a girl from stalking:

> There is a girl this year that isn't feeling very comfortable at all, because there is this one kid and she says he even followed her into the girls' bathroom one time. She has come to peer mediation to try to solve this and I think he just got suspended for a couple of days. She has cried out so many times.

A health teacher complains that the curriculum avoids complex issues raised by the policy. While physical education staff were instructed to teach a booklet on sexual harassment, she says they received no training and are unclear about what they can and cannot say. Current procedure is to have students read the booklet aloud without discussion. She is relieved that they were instructed to skip the page on adults' use of their power to harass students sexually, as this could, in her words, "open a can of worms." By this, she refers to forbidden uses of power and sexuality in adult-student relationships. More broadly, this "can of worms" might be seen to contain many issues put off limits for discussion with adolescents in school.

Peer mediation, facilitated by trained students with an adult observer, offers another approach to difficult issues including sexual harassment. The school social worker, on site part-time, reports, "At this age, youngsters often don't know how to talk to each other so they touch each other, often inappropriately." Peer mediators work to elicit more appropriate responses. The social worker runs a girls' group where girls bring issues ranging from boys to families to dealing with loss. They use role-playing to problem-solve various situations. In the process, she says, "[the girls] are becoming assertive, learning to say things effectively without being offensive."

Girls are also aware of another gender-based initiative by the school: the GESA staff development on classroom equity. Seventh-grade girls describe strategies used by teachers who have participated in GESA training. Some of these teachers have brought students in on the issues, creating a potential avenue for future student discussion.

> The English teacher, he really told us about [the gender equity focus]. He told us that's the reason why we're all sitting boy, girl, boy, girl. He wants us to be equal. And then he gives us equal amount of time to answer questions.

> My literature teacher, she picks us by picking a boy first, whatever, picking a girl first, and then the next time a boy and girl. She does it equally.

> I think it's really good because they're trying to make us equal and stuff.

Seventh-grade teachers consider their messages to female students. A math teacher wants to teach girls "to think for themselves, be your own person, ask questions"; to get involved in intramural sports "because I don't want it to be an all-guy thing"; to do well so they can be self-sufficient. Girls need to know, says the teacher, that "education can bring anything within their reach."

Glinnie's definition of sexual harassment is distinctly different from the broad and multifaceted one outlined by the policy. For her, there is a large and exciting realm of good, explicitly sexual interaction between girls and boys. Telling good sex from bad is not difficult: If you like the attention, it's good; if not, it's bad.

Mrs. Gordon describes an incident from her student teaching: She was explaining that she would be "flexible" about an assignment when a boy asked leeringly how flexible she was. She ignored him but later worried that girls would interpret this as passive acceptance. She wants girls to feel they needn't be quiet or "fade away" but rather that they can be "strong and outspoken without being labeled bitches."

Inequities That Trouble Girls. The principal describes seventh-grade teachers as "very gender sensitive." Eighth-grade staff will begin GESA next year. Meanwhile, eighth-grade girls critique both blatant and subtler forms of gender inequities they witness in their classrooms:

> In one of my classes we have a male teacher and when we play a game he's always, "Boys, come on!" You know. I mean, he always calls on the girls more but in the games, he's like, "Come on, you guys! I'll give them one more time."

> But I feel that in a lot of classes, especially with a male teacher, the girls get treated better but it's not educationally, it's more like a delicate...It's like some sort of stereotype that really needs like not to be there.

Despite a climate where girls and boys are gaining awareness of gender equity issues, girls at both grade levels continue to note inequities. For example, they say, gender-based assumptions affect students' choice of electives:

> People say, well boys shouldn't be in [home economics] because the boys don't belong in the kitchen.

> Some people say that [only] guys should be [in industrial arts] because they only do construction work and stuff like that.

Girls also point to an inequity that limits boys' choices in gym: While girls select wrestling or aerobics, boys all take wrestling. Girls are acutely aware of gender differences in athletics. They struggle with potential gains and losses of a separate but ostensibly equal system:

> In gym we have girls play with girls and boys play with boys because [otherwise] some people [boys] do all the work.

> Because now we're doing softball and if we put them together sometimes the boys just like pass to the boys because they know the girls won't [get someone out].

> In gym we're doing jumping. We have to jump as far as we can. And the girls are supposed to go five foot two or three inches and the boys' [goal] is higher. [I feel like] we're little mushrooms.

> When it was real cold outside, I think it had just rained, girls would get into their groups for [practicing] football [indoors], and boys had to go run extra laps [outdoors]. I noticed that. The reason why they did that is because they had the girls inside learning how to play football. The boys already know how. They went outside.

A number of girls at Madison express pride in their cheerleading squad, which, as they report, has earned more trophies than the (male) basketball team. They argue that cheerleading itself should be considered a legitimate sport and allowed to compete with boys' teams for preferred time slots, playing fields, and equipment.

These girls are raising questions about gender equity: Should girls and boys always engage in the same activities? Should they play together or separately? When girls have less expertise and body mass, should class be structured to compensate for or ignore such inequities?

Several girls who consider themselves outspoken make a link between gender and other issues of inequity in the school:

> I get really upset because if we're having this whole woman-man equal thing, then age shouldn't matter. I don't care if they're smarter than me, I don't care if they're older than me. If I have something to say, you're going to hear it. Because in the rule book, if they're going to go by the rules, it says teachers have

their right to explain their side of the story. If a teacher cuts me off, I'll go off because I don't like being cut off, I don't like being in trouble without getting my side of the story.

[When I speak out] I feel good about myself because [the teacher] has to hear me. If she doesn't want to hear what I'm saying, too bad. That's her job, to listen to her students, and that's what she's going to do.

These girls have defined their role as challenging power inequities by speaking out and insisting on a hearing. This stance is not without its risks, from censure in class to disciplinary actions.

The principal describes the eighth-grade student leadership as African American girls who are "verbal, confident, assertive, and united." In her estimation, these girls speak their minds. When five African American students approached her with a plan to celebrate Black History Month, she readily agreed. As a visible minority in the school, however, the girls were aware of their vulnerability as well as their strengths. Last year, a girl reported, "somebody put a swastika on my locker." As Black History Month approached, the girls worried, as one said, that "they had better not do nothing."

When a focus group of boys turns to a discussion of girls and boys in school, one boy describes Madison girls as "successful in school [because] they do more than guys in school," while boys' strength is "stand[ing] up for what they believe in." Another boy describes girls as "actors" and "traitors"—"impostors" who "just keep switching around [social] groups" and "change instead of staying the same." While these boys interpret girls' behavior as conforming, a girl describes her own behavior as "learning how to adapt to different people and different things."

At Madison Junior High, a predominantly middle-class, suburban school, adults in the school and the community strive to prepare "students—female as well as male—to enter a shifting job market, often via college. The school approaches equity issues in terms of widening access through visible policy and programs—for example, by instituting a schoolwide policy on sexual harassment that presumably frees girls to concentrate on their academics and by participating in a districtwide professional development initiative aimed at teaching teachers how to make their classrooms equitable learning environments. This approach, promoted by a female principal who names gender issues in school, makes gender equity an explicit and ostensibly schoolwide goal. On the other hand, both policy and program emanate from the top at school and district levels. Faculty involvement with these issues is uneven and neither girls' nor parents' perspectives have yet been widely solicited and incorporated. Ironically, the very order that helped to spawn policy and program at this site may also undermine a "messier" and more personalized process that would bring adults and students more centrally into discussions of gender in school.

School Snapshot

Name: Garth Middle School

Place: East Coast Urban

School Size: Approximately 1,300

Class Makeup: Predominantly African American

At 8:45 a.m. Sheree passes double-dutchers and a security guard to climb steep concrete steps. Pulling open the heavy metal doors, she enters the pre-Depression era building. An African American eighth grader, heavyset and yet agile, she moves confidently through the marble entranceway to her classroom. She wears her hair piled up with strands gold-sprayed, but her dress is casual—a flannel shirt, cords, sneaks. Once in the room, she joins a group of girls and boys talking excitedly to their teacher about yesterday's basketball game. Garth girls won even though the other team played rough and no fouls were called. A boy repeats his warning to the opposing team: "Garth kids ain't no punks; these girls can fight!" Sheree drops an invisible ball into an imagined basket on the way to her seat, back row and center.

Though ground level and dim, this room is bustling, with desks in rows but close together, materials for science experiments crowding available shelving, and a walk-in closet that serves as a changing and semiprivate area. These youngsters have been with each other and this teacher for three years in the Performing Arts House. Vanessa Sutton, a thirtyish African American woman with a rich smile, collects dioramas that students have constructed to illustrate the novel *Slave Dancer*. With no discernible transition, class has begun. Several boys without projects tease girls about theirs, and a girl in the front row cautions the teacher, "Don't show anybody!" Ms. Sutton responds, "Don't you let those male wannabes who didn't do theirs down your project! We gotta talk about this!" Sheree hands hers in readily, pointing out her ship's prow.

These youngsters represent the first graduating class from this "house," a small learning community founded by a handful of teachers committed to working with a stable group of students over time. A boy says that boys and girls in this class are "like brother and sister," working collaboratively on projects, though sometimes they also "go together." He recalls preparing for a class performance: "It was like, about nine or ten of us, and we all made the plot of the story and how we was going to set it up and then started doing dialogue....Half the class wrote the script and made costumes, and the other half of the room played the skit." These youngsters value invitations from their teacher to participate in extra activities like theater and law classes. They attribute their growth to connections with one another nurtured by a teacher who both listens to them and pushes them to meet high expectations.

Ms. Sutton is one of a number of adults at Garth who reach out to girls, discerning needs, helping girls develop their negotiating strategies, and providing academic and other supports. In a large middle school, the house structure lends itself to developing and sustaining such relationships. Even so, the needs of individuals—exacerbated by socioeconomic and racial inequities—often seem to overwhelm available supports. In this school snapshot, we will hear how girls and adults view the complex issues facing these adolescents, and we will look at supports that help girls negotiate school successfully. The snapshot will highlight the role of adults as girls' mentors and advocates in the context of an evident gap between supply and demand.

Gender in an Urban School: Girls' and Adults' Perspectives

During class time, nonteaching assistants—school staff who monitor designated areas of the building—question youngsters walking the halls. Between classes, the hallways fill with voices and bodies. Boys bump against girls and girls push back, to the sounds of laughter, arguments, and the banging of metal lockers. With a student body of more than 1,300—mostly African American but with a growing Latino population—Garth is the largest middle school in a sprawling urban district on the East Coast. To accommodate all the students, lunch shifts are staggered over several hours. The fifth-floor cafeteria is crowded and noisy; even those who forgo the institutional fare risk getting caught in a food fight. Girls sit with girls, boys with boys.

"Boys call you 'B' [bitch] and 'hoe' [whore] for nothing. I don't put up with it. I fight them. I used to like math but now I hate it. I'm so worried about everything else that I sit in class and panic and I can't remember my times tables."

Not atypically, "white flight" from this urban area has produced racially isolated schools and a dwindling tax base. While neighborhood girls and boys share a set of economic and social pressures, these pressures play out somewhat differently across gender. Many of the girls at Garth express anxiety about sexual pressure and early pregnancy. Their research questions reflect this concern. One asks, "Do boys respect girls enough to wait until they're ready?" Queries another, "What is it like for a girl with a baby at home to attend school?" Eladia recounts family history: "[My mom] was pregnant during school and she couldn't go back because of the responsibility. The same with my sister." Eladia wants to be the first female in her family to graduate from high school.

Gender "difference" may become gender antagonism, pressing girls to assert themselves in order to hold their own in relation to boys. Among themselves, girls talk heatedly about their sense of physical and psychological invasion, sometimes connecting this with academic achievement. Stacey explains, "Boys call you 'B' [bitch] and 'hoe' [whore] for nothing. I don't put up with it. I fight them. I used to like math but now I hate it. I'm so worried about everything else that I sit in class and panic and I can't remember my times tables." When a boy began following and threatening her in school, Eladia turned to her house director, a longtime teacher who invites in community members from such organizations as the Red Cross and a nearby university to help support "at-risk" girls. The house director intervened on Eladia's behalf: Says Eladia, "She talked to the boy and she told me, 'Don't worry about it. She'll take care of it.'"

Girls also acknowledge that their attraction to boys raises contradictions. At the end of a focus group in which girls complained passionately of boys' impatience and disrespect, a young woman poignantly voiced her own uncertainty about what she might decide in the moment with a boy she cared about.

A teacher who sees gender struggle as a critical dimension of classroom life incorporates the issue of "respect" into her curriculum:

> I try to let the girls know that the most important thing to remember is that they have to be respected....I see things happening in the classroom as far as cursing, disrespecting young ladies, and ladies disrespecting young men. I make [students] sit back and think about what they are doing. Talk about it. Write about it.

The principal, herself a mother of boys, witnesses what happens "when boys provoke girls": "I see [students] running down the hallway—he starts off, but often it's the girl who responds and gets in trouble." She has sought out the perspectives of several girls known to be tough and assertive. A tall, strong eighth grader with a reputation for fighting, Yvonne reports, "When [the new principal] asked me how I'd make the school better, I said, 'Try peer mediation.' She brought it in [and] I'm a mediator."

While both girls and adults seek strategies to lessen gender antagonism and promote mutual respect, girls also search for safe places of their own. The library—a sunny rectangular room with stacks at one end and worktables throughout—is a favorite place for Eladia, a seventh grader wearing a parka over her frilly white blouse. Several female friends agree. One explains, "We like to come if it's open. We read the stories [a friend] writes. Sometimes we read parts out—quietly."

The Key Role of Mentors. While Eladia and her friends have some success at carving out a space for themselves, an adult mentor can facilitate place and time as well as talk. Monica, a Garth graduate now at a magnet high school, also recalls the search for a quiet, safe place, especially during lunchtime. Her relationships with a few female friends and a caring adult provided this. "[Daria Burns] let us come down and eat lunch with her—nobody let us eat lunch with them, lunch is a time to get rid of all the kids— but Mrs. Burns let us come down and be with her." Ms. Sellers, a teaching aide who we met in Chapter Two, provided a room and shared times for girls including Keisha to sort through troubling issues. The room was lost this year to space demands.

Reflecting on the importance of older mentors for urban adolescent girls, Monica explains how she herself now strives to be a role model for her sister, a sixth grader at Garth:

> I try so hard to be successful because…my little sister looks up at everything I do. She be like, "Oh man I want to go to this party." I be like, "Don't you got homework?" She be like, "Yeah." "Well, do your homework first and then if you do it all right maybe then you get to go to the party." She be like, "Yeah. Yeah! You right." So she go do her homework. I have to be there for her and listen to her and do things so she can say, "I think I want to be like you."

A core of committed Garth adults—most often school insiders and African American women—look for ways to weave strong mentoring relationships into an already packed school day. These adults recognize that their support can help girls using "troublemaker" strategies to try out leadership roles. A Garth gym teacher who runs a group for "girls in trouble" invites in "black women who have made something of themselves so [girls] could see, 'Hey, I could do that or be that. I don't have to be in the street.' I came from a background like theirs—projects, welfare, I was a bad girl—and I tell them, 'Here I am, a professional woman making good money with a nice home.' That could be them and they could do more."

While less common, adults' mentoring of girls also crosses lines of race/ethnicity. Of her white homeroom teacher, an African American "special needs" student midway through a successful year comments, "I always had problems with teachers because I'm so outspoken, but [Caroline Walker] always understood it. . . . She always asked, 'Could you explain yourself?' She motivated me."

A Garth adult also makes a strong connection with a girl using schoolgirl strategies, which helps this girl to acknowledge and exercise parts of herself that often remain hidden. Identified as successful by teachers, Marilyn has employed a play schoolgirl strategy to negotiate a school culture that she assesses as different from her home culture. A Puerto Rican who is a minority in Garth's African American setting, Marilyn articulates succinctly the instrumental aspect of the good girl strategy:

> So this is the way it is: I may be bad on my block but when I come to school I'm so good. Because on my block it's the way the people act and the way they talk and they're almost just like me because I'm not really one of them girls that likes to be quiet and all. But when I get to school I act good and I pay attention to what I'm doing in school because I would like to be something in the future.

Marilyn is confident of her ability to use this strategy to achieve her goal: "Some of my relatives say bad things are going to happen and I'll end up like my sisters living on the streets and all, but it ain't going to happen. I am a very hard-working student."

However, her schoolwork shows an ability to summarize but not interpret or analyze; her ability to look successful may have hindered Marilyn from receiving the extra attention necessary for her to develop those high-order thinking skills. Marilyn established a solid connection with an adult as a result of her participation in the research. After the school-based researcher encouraged her to think critically about herself and her worlds, she explained, "I never talked [about my life] like this before, but it has always been inside of me to be able to do this, just no one ever asked these questions." Marilyn's school strategy—masking gaps as well as revealing strengths—reminds us that there is never enough adult time and attention to go around.

"I may be bad on my block but when I come to school I'm so good. Because on my block it's the way people act...and I'm not really one of them girls that likes to be quiet and all. But when I get to school, I act good and I pay attention because I would like to be something in the future."

Another girl describes a situation in which a teacher's approach undermined her self-confidence and the quality of her work: "They only picked a couple of seventh graders [for pre-algebra]. I could do it, but when the teacher tries to put me down, and I'm tender-hearted, then I'm not making it. My mom says she has the same problem, but it's my problem for not making it." She reports her conversation with the gym teacher, who coached her not to give up but to ask the math teacher questions that would help her grasp the material.

A special education student not only had failed to progress academically but also tried the patience of already overworked staff by lashing out physically and verbally at adults and peers. Teachers had given up on her when the elevator operator, an older woman from the community, entered the picture. The woman recalls:

Somehow the Lord put [the student] to liking me a little bit....The first thing was the math. The times tables. I had this book with these big times tables. And I started working. I would get that paper out and say, "If you don't want to learn, I'll learn myself." I would start like I was doing something with that paper. Then finally she came over and said, "Let me see what you're learning on." Every day I'd get that paper like I was really doing something. And she got interested. She learned her times tables. She got up to nine real good. It got so she would say, "What tables do you want me to do for you today?" I'd say, "How about two" or "You can do six." She was beautiful.

Sheree describes Vanessa Sutton, founder of the Performing Arts House, as "my school mom, I could learn in her class and I could also talk to her." But she also reminds us of the variability of adult-girl interactions. In a girls' group directed by Ms. Sutton, where youngsters probe everyday experiences and share strategies with the help of an adult, Sheree reflects, "Sometimes counselors don't help. You tell them what's happening and they sit there and say, 'What's wrong?' At one point I was trying to kill myself. She [the counselor] didn't care. I lied and said I was better so I could get outa there." Ms. Sutton leans forward on her stool and replies:

Life's hard and sometimes it just doesn't make sense. Each of you here has a strength, and you gotta find out what your strength is and use it to get out. You know what's the out for y'all—that's why I get so mad when you don't do your work. It's school. You gotta support each other. If Sheree doesn't hang with you today because she's going to the library, instead of saying she's stuck up, say, "Can I go to the library with you?"

Links Across the Gender Divide. As Ms. Sutton's words suggest, structures of race and class cut across gender so that in some respects African American girls and boys share more than either does with same-gender, middle-class whites. A boy in her class echoes Sheree's appreciation of relationships with strong, supportive adults:

> [The music teacher] is like a person I can look up to now, because he goes to church and stuff and he let us be us. Like no cussing and all but we get to talk, we get to talk like, "Man, get out my face," playing around. Mr. Wells don't mind that as long as we do our work. And I think that's one of the reasons that we do have good grades because Ms. Sutton don't mind either sometimes. When you let us be us we can get our work done, but if we got to sit there with our hands folded…

Nevertheless, the scarcity of resources may mean that girls see their needs losing out to those of boys. Says Sheree:

> Right now I'm in between my grandmom house and my mom house but most of the time I stay at my grandmom house so she can help me with my homework. We had a tutor come on Saturdays but I wasn't really into that 'cause my brothers needed more help [than I did] so again I was pushed to the side.

Fortunately, the strength of Sheree's relationships at school with her teacher and at home with her grandmother continue to fuel her academics and her engagement. Ms. Sutton's class brainstormed questions for their science projects: What is sound? What's the source of light and how does it travel? How do mice see? Do they see colors? Sheree was excited: "I can't wait to get to the experiment! Me and my grandmom do it together, we make a mistake and start over, make another mistake and start over, then finally we do it right." Months later at the project presentation, her posterboard asks in electric-looking letters, "How fast does light travel?" Her other research questions include "Does light bend and how much?" and "Did a man or a woman first do this research?"

Sheree's enthusiasm addresses several issues: First, a classroom setting where girls are comfortable to brainstorm science topics, particularly in the presence of boys, suggests trust and skillful facilitation. Second, Sheree has taken the classic scientific method of trial and error and brought it home. She's justifiably proud of how she and her grandmother tried and failed and tried again. Science class helps her learn life strategies as well as a method to conduct scientific experiments.

The Burden on Mentors. In an environment where teachers have leeway with their classrooms and programs, and committed adults can infuse gender issues into their curriculum, counseling, and teaching approaches, Ms. Sutton sponsored an assembly in which girls played the roles of women they researched. She pushes her eighth-grade girls to take algebra and struggles with the tensions between pushing and supporting youngsters as they prepare for high school. She describes adult-girl interactions in terms of mutual learning:

> The Red Cross lady was [in class] and asked, "Would you stay with a friend you learned was gay?" I said I didn't want people, because I was her friend, to think I was.... But the girls right away said, "Yes! She's the same person." They were out in front on this.

However, such an individualized approach often puts the burden on those who are already dedicated and overworked, and is unlikely to challenge the status quo with regard to what is taught and learned in school. In a focus group with girls across a number of grades and houses, one girl names a failure of the formal curriculum: "[In our science text] we don't see anything about black female scientists—you gotta go deep for that." Other girls agree that school remains dominated by male interests: Females are tokens at best in their course material, several male teachers give boys preferential treatment in class competitions and on trips, and class discussions seldom center on girls' concerns.

At Garth, an urban school where gender issues intersect with issues of race and class, a handful of committed adults provide critical support to girls who use a range of strategies to negotiate school. These adults acknowledge girls' strengths, help create contexts where speaking out can be a successful strategy, and coach girls to try out new approaches. The adults either share elements of race, class, and culture with their students or cross these borders to respect their girls' challenges. However, there are too few adults for the numbers of youngsters in need. As a result, for every girl like Keisha coming into her own, there may also be a girl like Marilyn doing school without demanding the extra notice that would help her continue to achieve when the going gets tough. Furthermore, while structures such as stable, themed houses support the work of these adults, additional kinds of supports are necessary to reach all students and to prevent the burnout of dedicated adults in school.

School Snapshot

Name: Avila Middle School

Where: Rural Southwest

Size: Approximately 500 students

Class makeup: 45% Native American, 45% Latino, 10% white

At 8:05 a.m. buses pull in with youngsters from towns and pueblos across the mesa. Sofi, a slight seventh grader with a spray of frizzy brown hair, talks earnestly with a boy who hops down alongside her from the bus. The classroom they enter is square and bright, filled with artwork. Sofi settles at the worktable she shares with two male friends because otherwise "other kids would copy our work instead of seeing they can be smart if they want to be." Her voice is soft, with a trace of the Spanish accent the native English speaker has cultivated in her desire to be bilingual, an aim she says is hampered by Spanish classes taught by non-native speakers who "don't care." She wants to learn the language of the great-grandfather who indulged her mother's taste for coffee in exchange for her reading the Bible to him in Spanish. Students gather materials to work on their *retablos*—regional folk art representing a set of collectively recognizable images. Sofi lays out her sketch of the head of a woman with nonwhite features and a beatific expression. She got help with the composition from her uncle, who does carvings she's displayed in class. "Was this cheating?" she wonders aloud. Uncertain of her skills, she hasn't decided whether to paint or carve, and she considers the help she can solicit from others to realize her vision.

Mary Jane Wells, a fortyish white woman who is a latecomer to teaching, stops by the desk of a girl painting Christ on the crucifix. The girl wants to spackle her background to give it relief. Ms. Wells shows her how to dip and then flex her hand to get the spackle effect in a tiny area. The girl's first try is clumsy, but she tries again and improves. Ms. Wells reflects that, with five boys and seventeen girls, "I kind of have a tendency to assume that I gear to teach toward the girls. . . . When I have work that needs to be done I will often send a girl. Will you go get the wheelbarrow? Will you get a pail of water?" She negotiated with the principal to keep this class for the four core subjects so she could play a more direct role in her students' lives. She reflects:

> [When] we go out and play basketball or kickball, it gives us down time where we can. . . . The girls, they fight. One day they're best of friends and the next day they're fighting. If they're fighting, they'll come stand by me and tell me what's going on. But if I'm teaching math all day, we don't have a down time.

A relative newcomer to the area, Ms. Wells brings into the classroom a wealth of nontraditional female work experiences, including a stint in the Army. Daily she communicates high expectations of her girls. In her classroom girls and boys alike

which rowdy boys take the teachers' time, regardless of innovative teaching strategies. "Reforms in this school," she says, "are more for the teachers than the students."

Perhaps out of their concern that reforms do not sufficiently address students' needs, adults at Avila are at work on a multicultural curriculum. The effort aims both to include material from students' cultures in the curriculum and to use knowledge of students' cultures to inform the way in which the curriculum is implemented. In the art project we saw as this snapshot opened, for example, both the art form and the hands-on teaching approach indicate the teacher's awareness of students' culture. Even so, there continue to be gaps between intention and enactment, as evident in Sofi's assessment of the Spanish instruction. Gaps also show themselves in cultural conundrums such as a white teacher's understanding that pueblos prefer not to expose their culture to mainstream school interpretation.

Making Conscious Choices. Attuned to the subtleties of difference in their cross-cultural community, the girls at Avila are particularly candid about their use of strategies and need for multiple identities as they struggle with the sometimes conflicting values of home, peer, and school cultures. Belinda, a recent Avila graduate who returned to the school as an aide, explains:

> With any kid in middle school, you're trying to find yourself, trying to find your identity. Do you want to go this way? Do you want to go that way? And especially as a girl, you have high school guys and older guys always coming after you, talking to you: "Let's go here, let's go there."

Seventh graders offer eloquent descriptions of the choices they confront: Will they be "schoolgirls" approved by adults, "cool girls" popular with peers, or "*cholos*" involved with gang culture? In a focus group that cuts across these peer divisions, they discuss what it means to be a "successful" girl at their middle school:

> You have to get good grades. And participate in your learning activities.

> But it's also cool not to participate. The teachers want you to get good grades but all the kids in the school [don't].

> You like have a mask. You put a mask on so people will like you. Because you don't want people to know who you really are. Like if you're uncool and they don't really like you, they won't be friends. You try to be rough and tough.

This last girl's description of the pressure not to be "who you really are" betrays her mistrust and alienation; she needs skillful use of strategies to negotiate this morass. Jenny Jimenez, a community activist known to students on a first-name basis, teaches a class called Straight Talk that comes to the school through the auspices of a community-based agency. Here, she encourages students to "unmask" and help each other deal with such issues as gangs, drugs, and violence. At a meeting of the school governance council, a body of staff and parents empowered to make decisions for the school, the principal raises the issue of girls wearing blue bandannas as a badge of gang activity. The council issues a temporary ban. The next morning in class Jimenez asks, "What's going on with girls wearing blue bandannas in their hair here?" When boys answer, she presses, "I want to hear it from a female." A girl explains, "It's not a statement about gangs but about attitude. They do it because they're just being like everyone else." She and a friend agree to see the principal to explain that here bandannas signify peer pressure but not gang involvement.

Another seventh-grade girl expects to be trying out new roles and identities as part of moving on to middle school:

> For school we got an open mind, good grades, participation, we've got the attitude, a certain perspective. You have to suck up sometimes, you have to be quiet, you have to know certain people, you have to try to be yourself, you have to be attentive, on task, you have to study a lot. And for the crowd you have to wear the right clothes, you have to have the attitude, you have to be willing to bully people, you also have to suck up to like your friends or whatever, you have to be outgoing, daring, you have to know certain people…and sometimes you have to be mean.

This girl suggests that role-playing, including efforts to be tough and cool, are just a normal part of growing up.

A program like Econopolis, which simulates the operations of a real town, offers youngsters the opportunity to try out different roles and negotiating strategies with peers in a socially protected, academically connected context. The mother of a girl whom a teacher describes as "a good student" but "very quiet" sees Econopolis offering her daughter an opportunity to recover strategies that recall her childhood energy:

> When Sandra was a toddler, she was so stubborn that I attended a workshop for parents of difficult children. The workshop leaders said the research indicated that these kids often turn out to be leaders…and I see that happening now with Sandra. This year she's the chief justice in the court in Econopolis. The boys give her a hard time because a girl is over them and because she's very precise with the rules.

Eighth-grade girls who have tried out different strategies both with and without the protective cloak of a learning activity like Econopolis reflect on gains and costs of their choices:

> The guys make fun of us if you get good grades.

> Oh yeah, they tease you, "Oh you are a schoolgirl" and all that stuff.

Yeah, sometimes [boys] try to get you to ditch class with them. And then if you say no, they go, "Oh we will go and find somebody else. You are no fun. I can get somebody else better than you." And then they come back and ask you for money. And then they are your friend again.

Gender-Aware Teaching Approaches. Gaps between adult intentions and girls' experiences may catalyze real talk and, eventually, real change. Eva Tenorio, a young Hispanic math teacher who is working to revamp the math curriculum toward active, inquiry-based learning as recommended by the National Council of Teachers of Mathematics,[31] uses her awareness of these gaps to inform her teaching strategies: "[Girls at this age] don't want to do well a lot of times, especially at math and science, because they worry about being perceived as nerdy and just into their work. So I look for ways [to help] the girls." One way she does this is by giving the girls a standard nurturing kind of activity unlikely to cause waves in the community: She has her students tutor younger children—a process that she says helps the tutors as much as the tutees: "Even if they're not getting the A's on tests, by explaining the math to younger children they're getting it. So later when they decide they want to do well in school, they don't have to say, 'Oh no, I missed two years of math,' because they have it." The girls view their tutoring as acting as helpers, but Ms. Tenorio is both teaching them math by having them explain it to others and assessing their math knowledge.

She also has students assess their own work in math. Many boys and even more girls assert that working in cooperative group settings helps them learn math. Like tutoring younger children, this peer work places mathematics in a social context. One girl reflects, "I learn best when I am in a group. That way if one person doesn't understand, someone else might." Another girl allows that the value of group work depends on the makeup of the group: "Whenever I take a seat with Caroline, Minda, and Norma, I don't do the work, but with Alice I do my work really well because we help each other and don't fight with each other."

For many of the girls, peer relationships can operate to support or inhibit school success. Two Hispanic eighth graders who were friends in elementary school employed different strategies as they moved into middle school to deal with tensions between school and peer culture. As a "schoolgirl/cool girl," Alicia managed to develop a "cool" social persona while also satisfying both her own and the school's standards for academic performance:

> Once you come [to middle school] everybody changes. You have to act tougher and you have to be cool. Plus the fact we're learning how to grow up and everything. Us girls we're liking boys and the guys are liking girls.... In fifth grade I had this really really good teacher. She was like really strict. Everybody else they didn't like her and I was the only one that would like admit that they liked her. After that she retired. Everyone started admitting that they liked her. Since I was already friends with everybody and know how to be friends with everybody, and I started doing my work, then I don't know, I just woke up I guess.

One of the challenges for Alicia is to separate various aspects of her persona; for example, she is hesitant to mix her groups of friends. While impressed with Alicia's work, several teachers describe her as "cold." Her writing teacher, on the other hand, feels that Alicia's "independence" as a writer and a human being will serve her well as she moves toward adulthood.

While Alicia was learning to balance her social with her school persona, her friend Sandra—now the chief justice in Econopolis—was taking a different tack:

> In elementary I had a friend who was really smart. She didn't have to study but I really had to work for it. I was always competing with her, then she moved away. After that I kept doing good. I like being the best, being the smartest and stuff....I was all depressed last year....One semester I had the best grades in the whole grade but everyone hassled me. But I got over it. Somewhere along the line I thought, my future, my grades.

Sandra describes coming to terms with some amount of social isolation as a consequence of her "ambition." That this remains problematic for her, however, is underscored by how highly she values a new friend, Anna, whom she invites to participate in the *Girls in the Middle* research.

I could be talking about something like consumerism, and out of the clear blue sky a student will ask me something about pregnancy. Well, I could just say that this is not the time, but it is the time, and I'll go ahead. Something has happened in that kid's life that this is a concern.

Avila girls have to negotiate not only the sometimes competing demands of peer and school culture but also the pressing imperatives of home and community. One girl's story of a critical moment in her struggle with dissonant home and peer values shows how an adult can both assert a parental position and demonstrate respect for the adolescent's need to try out strategies in the process of identity-making:

> Being smart is (knowing) what's wrong and what's right. I made my mistake and learned. Okay, in the seventh grade everybody was cool smoking. And I thought I would try it....And after that I kept on doing it....I was at a party. And when my dad came to get me, I smelled like it. My dad told me that if he ever caught me doing that again he wasn't even going to get mad at me 'cause he knew it was my decision and he can't be with me all the time. I told him I'm not going to do it again. I told my mom the same thing and she said she wasn't going to get mad at me 'cause she did it.

Belinda, the returning high schooler, reflects on how difficult it is for most adults to listen to and learn from the young people they purportedly want to help:

> The main thing kids do, they'll try to communicate to you, but you don't listen. A lot of adults will say, "We listen to you. You have to listen to us." And all this. At a youth thing I had done for a conference, our main question was, we wanted to know why adults say they listen to us but while they listen to us, are they really hearing what we're saying?

Nina Perez, the teacher of Family and Consumer Sciences who we met in Chapter One, does listen, putting aside her own teaching agenda as needed to address spontaneous but important concerns that arise in her classroom:

> I could be talking about something like consumerism, and out of the clear blue sky someone will ask me something about pregnancy. Well, I could just say that this is not the time, but it is the time, and I'll go ahead and I think it's important enough. Something has happened in that kid's life that this is a concern. So I think that's really important, especially for girls. I think guys will learn as much from listening.

She addresses gender issues explicitly, teaching girls to assert themselves socially as well as economically:

> For instance, we're working on consumerism right now and one thing I'll tell them is, I don't care if you do get married, you make sure you have your own credit references, you have this and that, to make them aware that they have to have their own personality, their own everything. [On the post-test] the boys still stated almost the same thing, only added a few more things I had taught, but the girls said the mother and father work together to help the family. And I said, "Good! You got it!"

A rap session with their teacher and a researcher offered sixth-grade girls a chance to think about the connection between academic achievement and harassment. As a reward for good work, they are permitted to select their working groups, which are usually all girls. This girls-only rap session allowed girls to explore incidents that had left some feeling uneasy with particular male classmates. Said one girl, "Well, sometimes I don't like to be with boys because they criticize you, like you can't do that because you're a girl." One girl explained, "[A boy] would always tell me, 'Why don't you come to my house after school and we could….' Then one time he told me, 'Well since you are in my group you're going to be doing all the work for me.'"

Girls value their reading/writing workshop as a place where an adult acknowledges their autonomy and creativity and takes their work seriously:

> You write something and…[the teacher] will tell you what your mistakes are, [then] you can rewrite it if you want to.

> She doesn't tell you you have to [write about] this or that or have so many words.

> Sometimes if she really likes [something you write] she'll give you like a book that has addresses of publishers.

> Sometimes she'll tell you you oughta enter it in a contest.

Underlying School-Community Tensions. In the communities feeding Avila Middle School, females are expected to play crucial roles in the home and the culture.

These roles may fit uneasily with school goals, which encourage young women away from family into higher education and the job market. In this context, school staff have shied away from challenging cultural norms. They struggle to reconcile the pulls of tradition with a fiercely modern present. The principal explains:

> Knowing that the girls are coming from very traditional backgrounds, I think it's a strength because they are a little clearer on who they are and how they are supposed to act. Which I can also see as being viewed as a real narrowing of options, from outsiders…and I sort of struggle with it, 'cause I was raised in L.A. but my parents are from here.

He predicts that a female colleague in district administration will hit a glass ceiling: "I could never see a female Hispanic in really high-level decisionmaking places in the state…well, probably a female, period, as a superintendent."

Most youngsters at Avila, boys as well as girls, share membership in groups with minority status nationally and live in a low-income area where economic prospects are shrinking. Native American youngsters in particular must navigate the complex cross-cultural terrain of pueblo communities struggling to maintain their integrity in the face of both Hispanic and white invasions. The middle school is part of the district's efforts to bolster minority student achievement by implementing developmentally appropriate reforms such as teaching approaches that use active, collaborative learning strategies. Addressing gender issues explicitly would challenge community norms, perhaps alienating segments of an already fragmented school community. A teacher like Ms. Perez walks a fine line, subtly raising gender concerns in relation to situations that emerge in the classroom.

In general, Avila employs programmatic middle school reforms that address gender in a variety of guises. For instance, reforms in curriculum and teaching approaches evident in Econopolis, a reading/writing workshop, Family and Consumer Sciences, and an interdisciplinary, hands-on math/science program increase the repertoire of activities and skills for girls and boys: A girl using a schoolgirl strategy carries authority as the mayor. A play schoolgirl's privacy is gently invaded as she is required to share writing with a peer. Girls hold and study rats and an iguana. Boys teach pre-schoolers and gain kitchen competence. Nevertheless, girls at Avila voice a sense of frustration and alienation that adults' efforts have yet to fully address. Without explicitly addressing gender issues as a facet of youngsters' lives and school reform, the school misses an opportunity to help girls analyze options and make strategic choices for the present and the future.

Implications

In Chapter Three we entered a suburban, an urban, and a rural middle school to examine the dynamic relationship between girls and schools around gender issues. Across these schools the girls share certain characteristics: All are adolescents; all spend large portions of time in the structured settings of schools; all are concerned with questions of identity; all import into their school lives elements from home and community; all have achieved some measure of success. But each commonality also incorporates differences: These girls are not all at the same stage of adolescence. The girls fashion their identities differently, reflecting home, peer, and school cultures. Also at variance are opportunities and constraints vis-à-vis gender offered by different homes and communities, and the kinds and degrees of success experienced by girls.

Schools, the other half of this yoked pair, are equally complex. Some have structures that explicitly address gender (like Madison's sexual harassment policy); some have structures that expand opportunities for girls without addressing gender head on (like Avila's Econopolis program). Schools all have education as their primary mission. How they reach that goal is helped and hindered by a variety of factors.

Madison, the suburban school in the Midwest, has received district support for policies and programs designed to achieve gender equity. But while girls describe teachers' performances in terms of their treatment of boys and girls in classrooms, these same girls have trouble naming adults in school with whom they share their concerns. Further, while many adults and girls agree that it is important to address gender issues in school, they bring different perspectives on the challenges girls face. For example, while the school implements a sexual harassment policy intended to protect its students, girls talk about how this policy can also inhibit them as they seek to negotiate their relationships with boys.

At Garth, the urban school in the Northeast, girls name adults and particularly women across all positions—from elevator operator to principal—who mentor and advocate for them. These adults seek out girls who are troubled, who speak out, who show promise. Girls appreciate recognition and acceptance of themselves and their strategies as they confront immediate issues like sexual pressure and safety as well as longer-term issues about their futures. But the demand for invested adults outstrips the supply. While girls report problems in their relations with boys, they also share with male peers the challenges of adolescence as configured by race and class. This suggests the importance of helping both girls and boys develop strategies that lessen gender antagonism and increase cooperative and mutually respectful social relations.

While Avila, the rural Southwest school, is engaged in a districtwide reform effort, its girls struggle with a community's low self-image that diminishes their abilities and prospects. Programmatic reform initiatives such as Econopolis that promote active, cooperative learning assessed by real-world criteria, and classrooms such as Family and Consumer Sciences in which the curriculum reflects a recognition of girls' experiences and dilemmas create contexts where girls can try out new roles and strategies. These reforms allow girls and boys to move into positions that demand the exercise of both traditionally "male" qualities such as independence and competence and traditionally "female" qualities such as interdependence and cooperation. However, gender issues are not made consistently visible, and girls continue to articulate the gap between their school lives and their real concerns.

The suburban, urban, and rural schools alternately promote and hinder gender equity as they handle specific gender issues such as sexual harassment, access to leadership positions, athletics, and safety and violence. For example, the suburban school's well-meaning sexual harassment policy would be informed by more open dialogue among teachers and students on what constitutes sexual harassment. In the urban setting, on the other hand, a policy defining sexual harassment and instituting consequences would address publicly worries that girls have acknowledged privately. In the rural school, a look at the issue of sexual harassment might provide a template for the governance council to begin to examine gender expectations and stereotypes.

All the schools need to increase access to leadership positions among girls across cultures and employing a range of strategies. Further, the school should encourage innovative reform programs such as peer mediation and Econopolis that foster leadership skills in girls who employ different strategies. Specifically, suburban schools need to work to develop leadership skills in girls who transgress rules and boundaries in order to learn from, rather than lose, these girls. Urban schools need to keep track of girls "doing school," offering them opportunities for leadership to stretch their capacity to speak out and gain visibility. Finally, rural schools need to help girls marginalized by race/ethnicity and/or class to take on positions as leaders who cross borders in these relatively isolated settings, though schools must be careful not to saddle these girls with so much responsibility that they have trouble fulfilling their own goals.

While a school's approach to gender equity emerges from the interactions and priorities of its adults and youngsters, it is also shaped and constrained by its position as an organization set in a larger community context. Chapter Four examines the interaction of girls and schools from the perspective of schools as organizations. It looks at the ways in which policies, programs, and invested individuals must converge in order to carry maximum benefit for girls and by implication for boys as well. Chapter Four suggests that public spaces where the diverse members of a school community can negotiate equity issues are crucial to institutional change.

GENDER EQUITY AND SCHOOL REFORM

In Chapter Three we looked at three school sites to examine the ways that girls' strategies of negotiation are ignored, challenged, supported, and expanded within a range of school settings. In Chapter Four we shift perspectives to look at gender issues through the lens of institutional change. Across the sites in this study, we found many separate individuals and program elements that support gender equity. But implementing reforms that make gender equity central to the institutional culture of a school is a difficult task. For schools with large minority populations, gender equity can be hard to disentangle from issues of race, culture, and economic class. Even in predominantly white, middle-class schools, prevailing gender roles draw from diverse political and cultural beliefs.

In the last chapter, we suggested that urban, rural, and suburban schools tend to approach gender most visibly in one of three ways: on the level of invested individuals, program development, or policy initiatives. In this chapter we look more closely at how these three levels can converge within individual schools to further the overall priorities of each school and the community that it serves.

Making Gender Visible

Gender issues do not disappear when schools do not address them directly: They percolate beneath the surface, seeking a place to vent. Openings for dialogue about gender can surface under cover of debate about such superficially unrelated issues as sports or race relations, as this section illustrates. Recognizing these opportunities can ignite the process of connecting individuals, programs, and policies to create a more equitable school.

This section examines how clashes in two different arenas—sports and race relations—sparked public inquiry into gender roles at two school sites. The first example involves a sports program for girls at Fairfield, a school in the rural South. The second case involves a public forum at Parkside, an urban school in the Northeast. While neither school explicitly addresses gender equity, each offers students and school adults a forum for challenging prevalent stereotypes about class, race, and gender.

Sports and Self-Command. At Fairfield, an athletic program puts boys' and girls' interscholastic sports on an equitable footing. Girls' games are important community events that draw large groups, cutting across class and race, and bring together parents, students, and teachers. Even though the literature on middle schools does not support interscholastic athletics, a Fairfield administrator argues that girls' basketball "is too important to our community to think about giving it up." At Fairfield, athletics offers adults an opportunity to challenge the prevailing stereotypes. And while Fairfield's athletic program does not explicitly address equity issues, it provides an opportunity to explore and critique traditional, regional expectations for "ladylike behavior," expectations that are often bound up with class and racial stereotypes.

Regina Jumel, an African American parent in this predominantly white school, told the following story (here recounted by a researcher) that illustrates how informal talk about girl athletes expands images of girls' roles and behavior at Fairfield:

> A teacher had telephoned Ms. Jumel to express her concern that her daughter, Natasha, an outspoken eighth grader, was developing an "attitude." Ms. Jumel explained to the researchers, "Natasha is very direct, and Southern women aren't like that." Ms. Jumel solicited the opinions of other faculty members about her daughter's behavior.
>
> According to the basketball coach, Natasha was confident. She explained, as an athlete "you need some cockiness, but that she does not have an attitude." The guidance counselor also noted that Natasha was unusually "mature" and wondered if this "was what the teacher was picking up on." Within several days of Ms. Jumel's inquiries, the teacher who had originally complained told Ms. Jumel that she thought she had previously spoken too strongly about Natasha's behavior.
>
> (From a researcher's field notes, 2/2/95)

This example suggests that even though talk about gender at Fairfield is often private and informal, the school community is characterized by contradictory expectations about girls' behavior. Because athletics is a prominent and respected activity at Fairfield, it acts as an important, if unacknowledged, catalyst for discussion of gender and gender roles. In this case, it even expanded the definition of acceptable female behavior.

Fairfield's participation in the *Girls in the Middle* study also generated a more public school discussion of gender issues raised by the athletic program. Through their observations and questioning, teacher-researchers at Fairfield prompted reflections on the community's contradictory expectations for girls.

For example, in a group discussion led by a researcher the day after a girls' basketball game, the following exchange took place:

> Classroom teacher: Stephanie is struttin' that stuff. She is a cocky little thing.
> Basketball coach: You have to have a certain confidence to play.

This exchange broadened into a discussion of the faculty's mixed reactions to girls who seemed sure of themselves and were leaders among their peers. Some members of the group were adamant that they welcomed strong girls into their classrooms. Other teachers disagreed, reflecting that confident and outspoken girls sometimes made them uncomfortable. The discussion, though cut short by time constraints, created an opening for further dialogue reflecting teachers' concerns and commitments.

At Parkside Community Middle School, an urban school in the Northeast, a recently established public forum generates dialogue across differences of class, race, and ethnicity. This dialogue has provided a site to air tensions in the multiracial school, which opened when a coalition of groups in this working-class community pressed for a new middle school to alleviate overcrowding and busing.

Race as a Gender Window. Parkside has explicitly encouraged discussion between diverse groups by inviting parents and community members to participate in the coordinating council, a schoolwide planning and development body. When a group of involved parents at Parkside complained that their community and their children were not being respected in spite of the school's stated commitment to cultural sensitivity, they requested a meeting with the principal and then addressed the entire faculty.

Marena Navarro, president of the Home and School Association and mother of an eighth-grade girl, explained why she thought it was important to speak out about issues of working-class and Latino identity:

> I sit on the coordinating council, but I'm not asked about curriculum, I'm not asked about budget. I'm told. The [teachers'] mentality is that everyone is on welfare. I teach my daughter self-esteem at home, but it seems like the schools do everything they can to lower the expectations of Latino students. The school is 41 percent Latino and they don't even send things home in Spanish.

Raising these potentially volatile criticisms provided an opening for parents and teachers to talk across their differences of class, race/ethnicity, and culture.

Gender issues were not addressed overtly in discussions between the Parkside parents and teachers. Yet staff members who were most connected to the community also provided the most leadership opportunities to their female students. Among teachers who had less understanding of the community, gender assumptions were deeply embedded in questions about student behavior. For example, some school staff admitted to the research team that they had misinterpreted or been puzzled by negotiating strategies employed by girls different from them in culture and race/ethnicity. Many non-Hispanic teachers were especially disturbed by working-class Latina girls who challenge middle-class norms of femininity. A teacher criticized Latinas as being "loud speaking, loud talking." Another teacher generalized that all the girls in the neighborhood—black, white, and Hispanic—lack ambition. Both generalizations are at odds with the views of parents in the community, who portray themselves as hard-working, if poor, people, who want their daughters to become self-supporting. Such parents' perspectives, which Parkside has begun to solicit, are crucial in helping educators understand girls' strategies and shape policies and programs accordingly.

Although still struggling, Parkside is working to shape a public space where parents, teachers, and other committed adults collectively build an urban school community. Several weeks after the open faculty meeting, Ms. Navarro expressed greater hope: "The principal wants to get the community involved. She was hired by the community. There are some teachers [who care], some faculty members. Maybe things will change."

Like the girls' basketball program in rural Fairfield, Parkside's commitment to community involvement is creating an arena for exploring gender across differences of class, race/ethnicity, and cultural assumptions.

Making Gender Issues a School Priority

As the above examples illustrate, it is possible for schools to begin to address gender issues without explicitly identifying gender equity as a program or policy goal. But naming gender equity as a school priority moves the process along immeasurably. Valley Stream Middle School, in suburban California, offers a good example of a site that can join individuals, programs, and policies to greater effect because it tackles gender head on.

Valley Stream, a large, racially and economically heterogeneous school, is located in a politically and socially divided community where a highly regarded principal promotes gender equity as a key feature of middle school program development. According to the principal, Fiona Tennyson, until recently students here were from the mainly white middle- and upper-middle-class neighborhoods surrounding the school. In 1993 the catchment area shifted, and the student population almost doubled to more than 1,000 students and became more diverse. Now about 20 percent of the students are Hispanic. About 25 percent of the student body receive free or reduced-cost lunches.

Although wealthier parents might have considered private school for their children, many continue to send their children to Valley Stream because of its honors program, its algebra classes for selected eighth graders who take the course a year ahead of the usual schedule, its prize-winning band program, and its racial and economic diversity.

Ms. Tennyson has worked to keep the school stable in the face of its growth. Her ability to maintain a safe and supportive environment is reflected in girls' perceptions of the school. As a seventh grader says: "Where I used to live, it was really rough, and that made the schools a lot stricter. Here they're really nice."

Another recalls: "In elementary school I felt like the teachers weren't being fair. Here no one's that way. Here it's really clean, and you feel safe here, and that's what they want."

Encouraging Personal Connections. At this site, programs, policies, and invested individuals converge to mesh gender equity with the overall priorities of the school community. This creates space for dialogue about gender in spite of the visible presence of antifeminist groups within the Valley Stream community. Drawing on the current literature about middle schools,[32] Ms. Tennyson underlines the importance of personal connections and self-discovery for young adolescents—girls and boys alike:

> The purpose of middle school is to expand each child's potential. Connecting with kids in a way that they know that they matter. Creating an atmosphere where there are activities.

> Special programming for girls fits right in. It goes back to self-esteem. Giving somebody a chance that doesn't have enough of a chance.

As elsewhere, the girls at Valley Stream were quick to identify the handful of committed individuals who made a difference in their lives. Girls consistently named Brenda Pappas as a teacher who addressed issues that were important to girls inside and outside of her classes. Ms. Pappas teaches several math classes that—while they are nominally open to all students—she designed specifically to meet the learning needs of young adolescent girls.

According to Ms. Pappas, middle school girls are "questioning so many issues— physical, emotional, educational." Although she says that "these are all middle school issues for both boys and girls," she notes, "I can't deal with all the issues all at once." Ms. Pappas links girls' intellectual needs to the social and emotional challenges of adolescence. Her classes include explorations of topics such as gender stereotyping, self-esteem, and career options. These equity issues are integrated with active learning strategies suggested by the state mathematics framework and the National Council of Teachers of Mathematics such as cooperative learning, use of hands-on materials, and real-life problem solving.[33]

Girls call Ms. Pappas at home, write her notes, visit her classroom during her lunch hour, and cry with her over a death in her family. They talk enthusiastically about Ms. Pappas and her classes:

> Before, I worried about saying the wrong answers and that boys would laugh. And in this class the girls don't laugh at one another and our teacher tells us to be supportive of one another.

> Like a lot of time she talks about things we don't really need for math but things that are important to us, but she talks about them anyway. Like she takes time for us.

Girls also named other faculty members whom they could approach with their concerns and problems: Carole Martin, a social studies teacher; Mary Sherry, a gym and health teacher; Gabriella Rivers, a counselor. Like Brenda Pappas, these faculty members developed deep relationships with students as well as programmatic initiatives that integrate gender issues into their work with young adolescents.

Social studies teacher Carole Martin explains that fairness is central to her philosophy of teaching: "Every girl and every boy should be given a chance to try. If they don't have the ability, at least they know they had the chance."

In keeping with feminist teaching approaches, Ms. Martin's curriculum units integrate women's history, academic skills, and active learning strategies.[34] For example, when Ms. Martin assigned a research project on the Middle Ages, one suggested topic was a comparison of boys' and girls' roles during that period. Half of the project was a formal research paper. The other half was a classroom presentation that could include role playing, period costumes, and food preparation. According to Ms. Martin:

> If you don't teach the history of women, you're not really teaching history. Even when I'm not teaching about famous women, I talk about things like why women used to have dowries. The boys in the classes usually start to appreciate all the work that women do in the home.

She reflects that even though some boys get "hard-line messages about traditional roles," most of the boys learn to regard girls more seriously.

Other programs at Valley Stream support girls in other ways. In physical education class, girls participate in weekly discussions on issues including self-esteem, nutrition, smoking, and friendship. A voluntary lunchtime rap group organized by Ms. Pappas provides a safe place to talk about issues like sexuality and teen pregnancy. The counselor also works with girls individually, conducts separate group sessions for boys and girls on topics like domestic violence, and organizes peer mediation.

First Steps Toward Healing Racial Tension. At Valley Stream, even girls who feel alienated from school name people and places in the school where they feel comfortable. A seventh grader explains, "I'm different than the rest of them. When you're a troublemaker, it's like totally different." Nonetheless, she says that through her training in peer mediation, she is learning to control her anger. The counselor names her as "one of the kids who pulls on my heartstrings."

African American girls, a tiny minority here, describe isolation and racism in the school. They ask, "Why can't they hire black teachers?" and one reports, "I'm the only black person in most of our classes. You have people looking at you because you're different." Several of these girls, however, say they like Ms. Pappas's all-girls math classes.

Hispanic girls, many of them daughters of Mexican immigrants, also talk about tensions they have experienced in the school. None of the Hispanic girls who met with researchers mentioned the absence of Hispanic teachers at Valley Stream. However, they did resent the school's unsympathetic response when the Hispanic students planned a walkout in response to a wave of anti-immigrant sentiment in the larger community. One seventh-grade girl recalled:

> **Before, I worried about saying the wrong answers and that boys would laugh. And in this class the girls don't laugh at one another and our teacher tells us to be supportive of one another.**

> There was this whole bunch of Mexican boys and boys in general. They started going up to where the buses are...and I was like, "You're gonna get in trouble" because I looked back and I saw one of the assistant principals.

Other girls, white as well as Hispanic, complained:

> They made rules against [the walkout]. That's not right.

> They locked us in our stinking classrooms because they thought we were gonna walk out.

While they were disturbed about the administration's response to the walkout, Hispanic girls spoke positively about Valley Stream and named teachers to whom they could turn for support. In addition, both African American and Hispanic girls are involved with the peer mediation program, and many of them have joined Colors, a group organized by the white counselor in response to charges of racism at the school.

At Valley Stream, visible policies that give a clear and unambiguous message about the need for gender equity enhance and promote the work of engaged individuals and their programs. The principal, Ms. Tennyson, vigorously enforces the school's sexual harassment policy, hires and promotes other women administrators, hires faculty members who are committed to gender equity, and supports teachers who develop programs to meet girls' needs.

Girls at Valley Stream recognize Ms. Tennyson as someone committed to gender equity and as a strong disciplinarian. Although many fear her, they also respect her. An eighth grader explains:

> This school is now getting more sports for the girls and allowing the girls to do more. The students know that Ms. Tennyson is trying to make this a more equal school; they know that she feels that this is an important part of growing up. She will come into the classrooms and talk to them about sexist stuff that has got to stop; if she hears of anyone saying sexist things, she will go to everyone's classroom and say this had better stop.

The first female principal of a secondary school in her district, Ms. Tennyson takes a strong feminist stance based on her own experience: "I really know what they mean by the glass ceiling 'cause I broke my neck on it....What it really takes is someone standing up and saying, 'I'm going to do this, and I will apologize later for the mistakes.'"

Members of the Valley Stream Middle School community do not all agree with the principal's ideology. Among the network of active parents at the middle school, organizational affiliations range from AAUW to the religious right. However, parents view the principal as a strong leader who provides a safe, supportive, and intellectually challenging environment for their children.

Ms. Tennyson has shaped an environment where young adolescent girls can expand their sense of self as they experiment with a broad range of negotiating strategies. Although the school does not adequately address the needs of its increasingly multi-racial student body, Ms. Tennyson and other faculty members have built on a long-standing relationship with parents and a strong middle school philosophy to create a public space for young adolescents to engage in ongoing dialogue about gender and gender roles.

How Individuals and Policies Can Bolster Program Initiatives

Valley Stream's example shows how programs, policies, and individuals can work together to make gender equity an overall priority of a school community. Valley Stream's example is not unique: All six sites in the *Girls in the Middle* study have implemented programs with the potential to integrate gender issues with other school priorities. In this section we examine these program initiatives as characteristic of middle school reform efforts. Then we consider how policies and people can join with school program reforms to make gender equity an integral part of a school's mission and culture.

It's no coincidence that the six schools studied share certain program initiatives, or at least elements of these program initiatives. In implementing these new programs, the schools have been guided by an extensive body of research that has followed the publication of the influential Carnegie report, *Turning Points*.[35] The "middle school approach" advocated by this report suggests that young adolescents, both boys and girls, share a set of developmental needs around connection, autonomy, and identity. Program innovations such as houses, team teaching, and cooperative learning are all intended to fill these needs.

Key themes of middle school reform—connection with caring adults and active engagement in learning—are also key themes in successful programs for middle school girls. However, until AAUW's publication in 1995 of *Growing Smart: What's Working for Girls in School*, the literature on middle school reform made only sparse references to gender issues.[36] In many ways this is a surprising gap, since so many of the developmental issues facing young adolescents involve understanding what it means to be a man or woman in our society.

Yet meshing gender equity with middle school reform is not straightforward: Often reforms that promote intellectually vibrant and emotionally connected schools frighten communities that are ambivalent about, if not threatened by, girls' intelligence, aggression, and passion. Although many existing school initiatives have the potential to support girls, they won't do so consistently in the absence of explicit schoolwide dialogue about gender. Likewise, in the absence of real talk about gender, the adults who work most closely with girls will remain isolated.

> **Meshing gender equity with middle school reform is not straightforward: Often reforms that promote intellectually vibrant and emotionally connected schools frighten communities that are ambivalent about, if not threatened by, girls' intelligence, aggression, and passion.**

Houses and Teams. One set of middle school reforms found throughout the six sites of this study help adolescents explore their growing sense of autonomy within a stable set of adult and peer relationships. These include structural reforms such as "houses" and "teams," which break up large, impersonal institutions into smaller subunits of teachers and students. Often students have a "core" teacher who spends more time with them and who students commonly identify as "my teacher." The house or team structure encourages teachers to work closely together, while it lets young adolescents experience moving from class to class without the anonymity that is typical of large junior highs and high schools.

At Garth, an urban East Coast school, the Performing Arts House (described in Chapter Three) has created a stable group of boys and girls who work collectively on such projects as research papers, theater performances, and science experiments over a three-year period. Eighth-grade girls themselves say they see the program encourage quiet "schoolgirls" to take on speaking roles and "bad girls" to begin to identify and strive toward serious goals. By creating a safe, familiar situation with a group of youngsters over time and encouraging their reflections on gender issues, Ms. Sutton

Some Reforms That Helped Students Deal with Gender Issues

REFORM	DESCRIPTION	WHY SUCCESSFUL	CONSIDERATIONS
Econopolis	Students select and play active roles in a schoolwide microcosm of society.	Encourages girls to take risks and try strategies that involve visibility and authority. Promotes cooperative work between girls and boys.	Can reinforce traditional gender roles if teachers are unaware of gender dynamics.
House or Team Structure	Links group of teachers with small, stable group of students over time. Sometimes features interdisciplinary teaching.	Promotes connections between students and teachers. Fosters supportive relationships between girls and boys.	Can stifle girls who relate poorly to "core" adult. Depends on adults' awareness of gender dynamics.
Girls' Spaces	Include formal classes geared to girls' needs and less formal groups in which girls discuss topics from relationships to career options.	Make a visible claim for the importance of girls' academic, social, and emotional needs. Encourage girls to develop autonomy in the context of supportive adults and peers.	Ongoing groups can provide a bridge to address the gender concerns of boys.
GESA (Gender/Ethnic Expectations and Student Achievement)	Staff development program designed to raise teachers' awareness of equity issues in their classrooms. Trains staff to work cooperatively to promote equity.	Makes issues of gender equity visible schoolwide. Promotes teachers' consciousness of gender dynamics in their own and their colleagues' classrooms.	Can encourage quick fixes, such as alternately calling on boys and girls in the classroom, instead of deeper looks at school gender dynamics.
GATE (Gender Awareness Through Education)	Staff development program funded by Pennsylvania's State Council for the Humanities in which teachers, administrators, and parents discuss gender issues in their school.	Encourages participants to pose questions and collect data on girls' school experiences.	Can be marginalized if not explicitly connected with other school programs and policies.

draws out quiet girls, encourages girls to speak out, helps girls translate between peer culture and school culture, and makes it cool to be in school.

Ms. Sutton's example reminds us that support from individual adults can be critical to making this reform work. But such support alone is inadequate to move an entire school toward dealing openly and equitably with gender.

Despite all good intentions, encouraging close and intense relationships between teachers and students can backfire. When these relationships are not backed by a schoolwide commitment to help teachers understand and expand girls' negotiating strategies, they can become exhausting, isolating, or even counterproductive for both girls and adults. For example, small learning communities can stifle girls if key adults hold narrow expectations about appropriate feminine behavior. Jessica, an outspoken white working-class girl in Fairfield, was repeatedly labeled "insolent" by her house teacher. Mona, an articulate Native American at Avila, was called a "troublemaker"—"a bright kid making some wrong choices"—and was engaged in an ongoing battle over discipline with her advisory teacher.

Teachers, too, can find themselves in deep water when they extend themselves unaided to help individual girls. Without a clear mandate from the school or support from their colleagues, they can find themselves confronting difficult issues alone. As one teacher put it: "It would be nice to have someone to talk to. It would be nice if I could go down the hall and say, 'I tried to do it this way today with the girls. How did it work for you?'"

This teacher's isolation was exacerbated as she received confidential letters from girls about their drug use and sexual activity. Although she believes that the level of trust she has developed in her classroom is essential to her students' development, this teacher not only worries that her girls have more needs than she can handle, but she also considers the risks she takes in violating her district's requirement to report any knowledge of student drug use.

In the absence of school policy and schoolwide awareness of gender issues, innovative approaches to teaching and learning can simply reinforce old gender roles, and structural reforms designed to foster a sense of community can increase tension and isolation.

Active and Cooperative Learning. A second set of reforms observed in this study focus on developing student-centered rather than teacher-centered classrooms. Student-centered classrooms encourage active learning through cooperative learning groups, hands-on experiences, role-playing, and thematic or interdisciplinary projects.[37] The authors of *Growing Smart* found that cooperative learning groups often support girls[38] and that hands-on activity is a key element in programs that successfully spur girls' enthusiasm for math and science.[39]

By facilitating connections and engagement, this reform can validate a broader range of girls' strategies and make these visible. As we saw in Chapter Three, the Econopolis program at Avila in the rural Southwest uses an active, cooperative learning approach to create a schoolwide microcosm of society that encourages students to try out new roles. In this setting a "play schoolgirl" becomes judge, discovering leadership and ambition that are buried in her usual persona. A "schoolgirl" takes on new visibility and authority as mayor. A "schoolgirl/cool girl," ordinarily preoccupied with fitting in, dares to challenge wayward peers in her role as crime stopper, and a "troublemaker" used to holding herself aloof becomes involved with media production. With the help of this program, girls and boys don and shed new approaches like snake skins in the process of adolescent identity-making.

However, the *Girls in the Middle* study also supports findings in the literature that cooperative learning groups can reinforce stereotypes of male activity and female passivity if teachers are not aware of gender dynamics among their students.[40] In one typical observation of cooperative learning groups, a researcher made note of two seventh-grade girls who exchanged knowing glances but did not speak as their male team member confidently proposed his strategy for solving a nontraditional math problem.

Similarly, unless teachers use their knowledge of gender dynamics in their classrooms to structure and monitor hands-on activities, boys often grab limited resources or feel more comfortable experimenting with new materials.[41] For example, in one school in this study, eighth-grade honors math students are encouraged to explore geometry with hands-on materials. Yet only the boys go to the back of the class to experiment with the wooden "Soma" blocks.

Professional Development on Gender Sensitivity. Programs that help teachers develop their sensitivity to gender issues in the classroom represent another set of school reforms that have developed in recent years. At least two of the schools studied for *Girls in the Middle* have such programs in place. However, the impact of these programs has been lessened by their conceptual and structural separation from other aspects of the middle school curriculum. Observations of several programs geared directly toward gender equity suggest that integrating gender into an overall approach to middle school reform can catalyze change, promoting public dialogue about such differences as race, class, and politics.

For example, the GESA (Gender/Ethnic Expectations and Student Achievement) program at Madison, a Midwestern suburban school, raised schoolwide awareness about the need to give equal classroom time and attention to boys and girls. Teachers who had participated in the GESA training made an effort to call on boys and girls in an alternating pattern. Together with the school's strongly enforced sexual harassment policy, GESA gives a strong message that girls are equal to boys, not second-class citizens.

On the other hand, Madison, still called a junior high school, has only recently started on the path to middle school reform. In spite of the school's highly visible focus on gender equity, girls at Madison do not describe the same close connections with adults that are important to girls at other sites. If gender equity meshes with middle school reform at Madison, teachers will become more deeply involved with their students, begin to experiment with programming that encourages girls to try out new roles, and start to develop curricula that present expanded images of girls and women.

At this point, the GESA model fits with Madison parents' hopes for workplace and career equity for their daughters. However, if gender continues to move into the center of Madison's institutional culture, new forms of dialogue could open up gender issues that fit less easily with current perspectives. The data from this study, like the literature, suggest that when adults begin to connect with girls, they begin to confront deep-seated cultural assumptions about femininity, including issues of female anger and female sexuality.[42] Just as schools need to create public space for the discussion of gender across differences of class and race, they also need safe arenas for dialogue about gender across differences of age, culture, and politics.

Garth, an urban East Coast school, is another site where gender equity and other aspects of program development are not yet fully aligned. Here a group of teachers are involved in GATE (Gender Awareness Through Education), a teacher research project funded through Pennsylvania's State Council for the Humanities. This program encourages teachers to examine what their female students experience in their classrooms and schools by posing questions about gender that have arisen in their ongoing work with young adolescents.[43]

At Garth, a handful of committed adults provide important supports to girls and develop innovative programs for their students, both male and female. Yet GATE is almost invisible at Garth, disconnected from other school programs and policies. Garth provides citywide connections for staff committed to working on gender issues, but needs to provide more effective institutional support for these adults within the school. Halfway through the GATE project, one of the two male teachers dropped out, and several remaining participants felt that other problems in the school left them little opportunity to focus on gender.

Gender issues are not treated as a priority in Garth's reform initiatives although they bubble up every day in hallways, classrooms, and the cafeteria. At many urban schools like Garth, parents and community members are committed to girls' achievement. However, in a community where most children, both boys and girls, face the obstacles of racism and poverty, adults are concerned that all their children need the opportunity to experience a safe, respectful, and academically challenging school environment. This suggests that if gender equity programs are to have a deeper and more sustained impact at schools like Garth, gender equity has to be integrated into a coherent policy framework that addresses other forms of inequality. In addition, gender equity has to be part of a programmatic framework that is connected to other schoolwide goals. On a local level, this means that staff, parents, and community members need to identify how gender issues intersect with other school priorities. For example, a team of teachers might decide to focus on sexual harassment as one aspect of creating a safer, more nurturing environment in their school.

GESA at Madison and GATE at Garth both provide useful starting places for developing gender-oriented programming. However, neither program has catalyzed the kind of connections between individuals, programs, and policies that are needed to make gender equity a school priority.

Time Out for Girls. Across all six school sites studied, the most common program reform that supports girls was "girls' groups"—classes and activities where all students are female. In these groups or classes, run by counselors, teachers, aides, or outside adults, girls discuss a range of concerns, from physiological changes to health care, professional options, academics, parents, boys, and abuse. At least on a short-term basis, girls' groups appear to encourage girls to develop autonomy with the help of supportive adults and are places where girls can address and even argue through their differences. As one girl explained, "We can say what we want. We don't have to worry about what the boys will say."

For the most part, girls' groups fit into the periphery of school organizations and are neither highly visible nor highly controversial. However, at Valley Stream, teacher Brenda Pappas instituted a math class and a forum for girls that made a highly visible and controversial claim for the importance of academic space for girls. As a reform that meshed gender equity with a developmentally appropriate approach to mathematics education, this class gained support from parents and administrators throughout the district at the same time that it generated increased dialogue about gender and equity issues throughout the school.

Implications

The examples discussed in this chapter suggest that school communities in rural, urban, and suburban areas are beginning to engage in dialogue about gender and gender equity in forums that are both formal and informal. Rural Fairfield and urban Parkside are examples of schools where invested individuals are beginning to challenge local assumptions about class, race, and gender. At suburban Valley Stream, this type of dialogue has begun to permeate the school as gender equity merges with middle school reform. While most of the schools in this study have not yet merged gender equity into their overall approach, they do have many programs in place that are already generating increased awareness of girls' needs and their negotiating strategies.

The data from this study suggest that gender equity can become central to the culture of a school when invested individuals, program development, and policy initiatives mesh to promote multiple spaces for dialogue about gender. This happens when:

- committed adults take risks, work closely with girls, and also build coalitions and support networks;
- program development makes gender issues visible in classrooms and schools, and embeds gender within an overall approach to the developmental needs of adolescent boys and girls; and
- policy initiatives highlight the centrality of gender equity to the school mission.

OUTCOMES AND RECOMMENDATIONS

This report illustrates and documents patterns that, on the basis of broader knowledge of research on schools and on gender and education, we have reason to believe are not limited to these six schools. In this final chapter we highlight the major outcomes of our study and offer recommendations about what those involved with middle schools can do to bolster the success of young adolescent girls.

As an important note, our research confirms what much of the literature[44] suggests: that reforms that are good for girls—such as small learning communities, close connections with adults, cooperative groups and active learning, and curriculum that builds on students' experience—are good for all students. Making gender equity an explicit aspect of the middle school reform agenda will strengthen education for girls and boys.

> **Girls in middle school use a set of recognizable strategies as part of the process of forming identities and negotiating school challenges. The strategies are subject to adult interpretations, so that what is valued as "leadership" in one school may be labeled as "troublemaking" in another.**

To allow for differences in school cultures and in ways of putting these learnings into action, our recommendations tend to be broader than the rest of this report. To suggest ways to implement the recommendations, we offer examples of actions that address gender equity at district, school, and classroom levels. For school staff, students, parents, and community members as well as policymakers and education professors and their students, the examples represent a menu of possibilities to meet the challenges of their own educational settings. These examples are intended to stimulate rather than inhibit the activist imagination seeking to create more gender-equitable schools.

Outcome #1

Girls in middle school use a set of recognizable strategies as part of the process of forming identities and negotiating school challenges. These strategies we call "speaking out," "doing school" in expected ways, and "crossing borders" of gender, age, and culture. The strategies are subject to adult interpretations, so that what is valued as "leadership" in one school may be labeled as "troublemaking" in another. Girls' success in using these strategies depends partly on how well their identities and approaches match the dominant culture of the school, especially in terms of race/ethnicity and class. Girls who don't belong to a school's dominant culture can succeed, drawing on the support of peers and adult mentors as well as on their inner strengths. Success at this stage is fragile for all girls.

Recommendations. Schools need to recognize girls' strategies and expand their set of accepted behaviors. Recognizing them and understanding that girls need to experiment with different strategies as part of their developmental process helps adults consider girls' strengths and needs as learners. Without this understanding, adults may rush to judgment—mistaking "negative" behaviors for causeless defiance or hormonal imbalance and clashing with girls whose strategies make adults uncomfortable. Thus adults may fail to tap girls' potential for leadership and growth.

Matching individual girls' strategies—particularly nonconforming strategies—to the right school programs and outlets for their energy can help girls mature and make a more positive contribution. For example, encouraging outspoken, even confrontational girls to be peer mediators can help them feel valued and give them a stake in the system they are used to attacking. Similarly, encouraging quiet, almost invisible schoolgirls to tutor younger children or take on roles of authority and visibility in a model town like Econopolis can prod them into articulating their values and inspiring admiration. Girls who cross borders and translate for others need support to manage the balancing act required of them. Adults can provide this support by encouraging the use of schoolwide dialogue journals and other approaches that explore student experiences and promote real exchange between adults and girls.

Outcome #2

Nothing is more important to girls' developing sense of self than a mentor. In the absence of well-devised programs to confront girls' identity issues, mentors play a critical role. Even where such programs exist, the interest of caring adults can be a key factor in whether programs succeed or fail in reaching girls.

Adults who share race/ethnicity, culture, and/or class with girls may have an edge in understanding girls' challenges. This does not substitute for listening to girls' versions of their experiences. Adults who build relationships with girls over time can help them make sense of their multiple and sometimes conflicting roles. Caring adults also bring high expectations. In interviews and focus groups, girls named these adults—almost always women and ranging in position from aide to teacher and principal—as critical to their success. Girls in Ms. Sutton's Performing Arts House at Garth credited their teacher as much as the program with helping them reassess their educational goals.

> Nothing is more important to girls' developing sense of self than a mentor. In the absence of well-devised programs to confront girls' identity issues, mentors play a critical role.

Girls respond differently to programs and individuals, and some girls may resist being mentored by adults designated for this function. "Real" encounters may be encouraged by allowing for girls' choices.

Recommendations. Bolster school support for adult mentors. These adults represent a cross-section in terms of position in the school as well as race/ethnicity and social class. Adults who devote extra time, caring, and energy to mentor girls need structures and networks—both inside and outside school—that recognize and support their commitment. Here are some strategies for supporting mentors:

- Schedule time for mentoring work so that it is not always relegated to lunch and after school. Also arrange for interested adults to work together. Structures such as "houses" within schools that link academic disciplines such as science and history and help adults know the "whole child" aid in these endeavors.

- Secure funding for this work to legitimize its importance and its time and place in school.

- Provide opportunities for mentors to receive public recognition and compare notes with other mentors both within and outside their schools. Professional organizations and conferences where gender issues are highlighted can function as arenas for feedback and sites for consultation.

- Help mentors protect themselves. Provide relevant legal information such as parameters for dealing with controversial material with students and guides to social service resources. Create opportunities for mentors to exchange information about their experiences and concerns.

- Lighten the loads of "insiders" by connecting them with adults in the community who can also enter schools to act as mentors, models, and advocates for girls.

- Offer girls more than one possible adult connection. Make sure their choices include an adult familiar with their culture who can "read" their behaviors and advocate for them in school.

Outcome #3

To achieve equity and empowerment for all students, school reform must be connected to girls' and boys' adolescent experiences and developmental needs—both distinctive and shared. While middle school literature recognizes the need for schools to help adolescents with developmental challenges, traditionally schools have placed a higher value on imparting academic skills. Identity development and academic skill-building should not be segregated. Rather, identity development should be recognized as involving skills that schools can teach girls as well as boys; some of these skills are distinct to boys or girls, while others are shared.

Recommendations.

- Make girls' experiences visible and important in school. Provide opportunities for girls to share concerns about their changing bodies, career goals, and relationships with boys, girls, and parents. Sometimes, separate spaces provide a safe context for this kind of talk. Although in daily life girls sometimes feel as if they are their negotiating strategies, they need opportunities to articulate these strategies as choices that they can revise. In doing so, they also help adults learn about female students. Likewise, boys may need such settings to deal with gender issues such as definitions of masculinity.

- Encourage innovative reform programs that offer girls and boys opportunities to develop new skills. Middle school reforms that stress active, real-world learning help youngsters struggle with developmentally critical issues of autonomy, role playing, and responsibility. Such programs promote equity most when teachers make equity issues explicit—for example, by encouraging girls and boys to try out nontraditional roles and activities.

- Open dialogue on gender issues in the classroom. Discuss gender as an aspect of students' lives, curricular materials, and classroom dynamics. Don't restrict the discussion to classes such as Family and Consumer Sciences, which deals explicitly with female and male roles, but encourage them whenever the curriculum or classroom interactions warrant. Gender issues are often tied to cultural issues. Use curricula and materials that show females and males from various cultures in a variety of roles.

Outcome #4

Leadership opportunities bolster girls' competence and sense of efficacy and increase their actual influence in school. School staff, programs, and policies need to encourage leadership opportunities for girls from all cultures—girls employing a range of negotiating strategies. Girls' leadership qualities need to be re-examined in the context of race and culture. Girls who cross borders as translators and schoolgirls/cool girls, and girls who stand up for their beliefs as maverick leaders are especially valuable as leaders in school reform. These girls can help bring multiple student voices to the school reform table.

Recommendations.

- Encourage programs like Econopolis and girls' athletics that—aside from their academic merits—foster girls' leadership skills and allow students to try out new roles.

- Expose girls to women in visible leadership positions, especially in the school and local community and across lines of race/ethnicity and class.

- Invite girls who use nonconforming strategies to take on leadership positions that will channel their insight and energy toward collective interests.

- In the classroom, use active, innovative teaching approaches like role-playing and cooperative learning groups that expand leadership opportunities, and discuss with students how to employ these approaches to expand both girls' and boys' repertoires.

Outcome #5

Suburban schools tend to approach gender issues through explicitly framed policies, urban schools through committed individuals' connections with girls, and rural schools through middle school reforms that seldom make gender issues explicit. But they all face distinctive challenges in achieving gender equity. In accord with their differences, individual schools need to become aware of their approaches and borrow approaches from each other in order to create an environment rich with possibilities for both genders.

Recommendations. Schools can learn from each other.

- Suburban schools need forums where girls and adults can discuss their concerns and modify, if necessary, policies and programs designed to support gender equity.

- Urban schools need a policy framework that makes gender equity a clear priority while connecting it with paramount community issues such as making schools safe and alleviating racial and economic inequities.

- Rural schools need to make gender issues explicit so that adults and youngsters can examine stereotypes and open up choices for girls and boys.

Outcome #6

Schools and school communities must mesh policy, committed individuals, and program reform to make gender equity essential to a school's priorities. Middle school program reforms already in place have the potential to address gender issues for

> **Reform initiatives must send an unambiguous message that gender equity is important to a school's mission.**

youth, but this potential often goes unexploited when schools fail to raise these issues explicitly as they occur—whether in the classroom, the hallways, or on outdoor school grounds. Reform initiatives must send an unambiguous message that gender equity is important to a school's mission. Reforms must also be varied or textured enough to validate and support girls who use a range of negotiating approaches.

Recommendations. Make gender issues visible at all levels—in districts, schools, classrooms, and hallways. Policies at state and district levels bolster the visibility of gender issues at the school level. Too often, policies and programs come from adult culture and do not address issues from adolescents' perspectives. Girls and boys must be included as partners in reforming schools to achieve gender equity.

All policies and programs have an implicit gender component that should be considered in design, assessment, and personnel assignment. For example, restructuring schools into small learning communities sets the stage for relationships between adults and girls over time; such structural change should acknowledge differences among girls when matching girls with personnel.

Outcome #7

Public dialogue, whether in school forums, assemblies, or debates, is critical to promoting and sustaining deep change in school. Schools that create regular opportunities for the airing of equity issues by students, parents, community members, and school staff are better equipped to understand differences, set priorities, and win cooperation on goals that mesh with community values.

Recommendations. Create public forums in which all segments of the school community—adults and students—can meet to address equity issues. Youngsters and adults often view the world from different cultural frameworks and receive conflicting messages about gender; exploring these areas of difference can be enlightening. Over time these explorations can help shape policies, programs, and interpersonal dynamics that promote equity.

The ability to appreciate diverse perspectives contributes to the success of girls who cross borders. All youngsters can benefit from learning this skill. Further, adults who grow adept at cross-cultural listening and translating are more able to help vulnerable students.

Outcome #8

Conducting research on gender issues is an often-overlooked strategy that can benefit girls in all school settings—suburban, urban, and rural. School research can be an intervention, a catalyst for positive change. In case after case, we saw the research we were conducting with girls and teachers generate attention to the issues and stimulate girls' development. For example, at Avila the girls' research group continued as a girls' writing group after outside researchers left. At Fairfield adults began a dialogue about their own experiences of gender, race, and class. At Garth students continued to consult informally with the school-based researcher. Generating inquiry into gender can open up a rich and provocative set of issues and help to create public forums for dialogue in schools—for girls and boys and for their teachers, administrators, and parents.

Recommendations. Research is an intervention when the inquiry process provides space and impetus within schools for students, school staff, and parents to raise questions and explore issues related to gender. Members of a school community can gather quantitative data by examining student achievement by gender, race/ethnicity, and socioeconomic status. They can also gather qualitative data by seeking and recording the diverse perspectives of students, teachers, and others. Even when a school cannot implement all changes advocated by participants, it can stimulate progress simply by creating meaningful opportunities for inquiry and communication across various groups.

Sample Actions at the Levels of Classroom, School, and District

- Form an ad hoc committee of students, parents, and school staff to examine how well the school is meeting the needs of girls using the range of strategies described in Chapter Two. Include race/ethnicity and class along with gender as lenses for understanding how the school can better support learning for all students. Consider what the school is already doing that might be modified to better meet needs of girls and boys.

- Use Howard Gardner's theory of "multiple intelligences"[45] to structure a social studies course unit in which students try out different approaches to their worlds. Gardner argues that we all have multiple intelligences, from the linguistic and mathematical/logical ones usually exercised in school to others such as the musical, kinesthetic, and interpersonal, often overlooked in school. Within these multiple modes of learning, girls and boys can practice a range of learning strategies that fall both inside and out of traditional gender roles. Teachers and their students in such a course unit could also discuss Gardner's framework in terms of how multiple intelligences relate to issues of gender and schooling.

- Create a professional network in the school district where adults can share the triumphs and frustrations that arise in their work with girls and gender issues. The network might be a setting for inquiry, such as at the GATE program at Garth. This kind of network can also stimulate coalitions among staff, joining aides, counselors, and teachers, for example, in an effort to support girls and promote gender equity.

- Encourage teachers interested in gender issues to plan and implement a cross-disciplinary unit together. A house or team setting in which teachers already work together and with a set group of students provides a ready-made site for this work. Consider including students in the design of such a unit.

- Encourage school staff to set up a formal, ongoing connection with a community organization, such as the local AAUW branch, that would involve them in working together to mentor groups of girls. Use the connection to help meet girls' needs to relate to adults from a range of backgrounds and in a variety of career roles.

- Invite girls to participate in district and school leadership, including governance committees, so they can gain experience as educational decisionmakers. Include girls who are confrontational and speak their minds, quiet girls who have been observing and reflecting on school, and girls who are adept at negotiating multiple cultures.

- Encourage girls who are "doing school" to take on speaking roles in the school and classroom, such as peer mediator, student government delegate, and speaker in cooperative learning settings. Build recognition for these roles.

- Form a group of students and adults to assess the needs of girls in your school. Both insiders and outsiders can then offer activities to meet these needs, for example, a writing group, a career forum, a group for young women of color.

- Devise curricular units or programs that require students to take on a variety of roles, for example, re-enacting historical events or opening a school store. Give students leeway for choice and encourage them to try out different roles over time. Talk with students about gendered role divisions.

- Identify school goals that intersect with gender issues. Build a coalition of students, parents, and school staff committed to integrating gender equity into school reform. Involve this group in reviewing, initiating, and monitoring policy.

- Advocate for district policies requiring incoming teachers to have had course work dealing with issues of gender, race/ethnicity, and class.

- Design a program that considers gender issues while it builds girls' math and science skills. Have the program integrate girls' developmental and intellectual needs.

- Design study units that involve student research into issues of difference including gender. Students can conduct inquiry into gender issues through surveys, interviews, and focus groups.

- Examine measures such as grades, test scores, and portfolios in terms of girls' and boys' achievements over time. Conduct interviews and focus groups with students to understand their achievements and consider directions for change.

See Appendix C, D, and E for suggestions on conducting research into gender.

AN EDUCATIONAL EQUITY INVENTORY

Use this list as a starting point to assess your school's work on gender equity. Taking inventory is a first step in a cycle of assessment and action.

Does your school have...

- policies that make gender issues a priority?

- supports for girls of all races, languages, negotiating strategies, and physical abilities?

- adults with whom girls can talk about issues such as sexuality, birth control and, family and peer pressures?

- support in the school and the district for adults who mentor girls?

- equitable athletics programs?

- a sexual harassment policy?

- data that show student achievement by gender?

- professional development to help teachers make their classrooms more equitable?

- curricula and teaching approaches that encourage girls and boys to try out a range of roles in the process of identity development?

- adults and programs that offer leadership opportunities to girls of diverse cultures who use a range of negotiating strategies?

- girls, parents, and school staff involved in assessing the school experience for girls and in shaping reform?

- forums for dialogue across the various constituencies of the school community?

Conclusion

What works for girls in middle school? How do girls themselves negotiate their schooling in the challenging transition from girlhood into adolescence? To address these questions, we have heard from middle school girls—African American, Hispanic, white, Native American, and Asian American girls from a range of socioeconomic backgrounds and achievement levels—as well as from boys, teachers, principals, and parents with whom these girls cross paths daily. We have visited middle schools across the country, traveling from the inner city through the landscapes of suburbia and to the outer reaches of rural bus routes. We have witnessed programs where girls take risks, try out new roles, and blossom as young mathematicians, athletes, scientists, and court justices, with the help of people and policies supporting their efforts. We have also witnessed girls' ongoing struggles to achieve success in academic and other realms, in the face of a society where young women, and particularly young women of color, continue to face bias and constraints based on their gender and race.

This report suggests that what works to support the success of middle school girls is congruent with sweeping national reform strategies, such as breaking schools down into learning communities where adults and youngsters know and care about each other, promoting active, cooperative learning strategies, and developing an interdisciplinary, theme-based curriculum that engages student's concerns. The overlap between school reform and gender equity is considerable. However, the danger remains that educational reform will continue to paper over issues of gender equity. Rather, gender and other equity issues must be made visible in order for school reform to achieve its ends. Each school's reform agenda must encompass the people, policies, and programs that create equitable educational opportunities and offer the public space to disseminate and debate these. Only then will girls of all backgrounds and the widest range of negotiating strategies be assured of the opportunity to author themselves.

A P P E N D I X   A

Research Approach

This qualitative research study was designed to illuminate how young adolescent girls experience middle school and how schools influence girls' experiences. It also investigates how differences (for example, race/ethnicity, class, ability/disability, community) work to shape girls' experiences of school. By using qualitative methods to explore adults' and young people's perspectives, we are able to examine gaps between what researchers and educators think might or should work for girls and what girls themselves perceive as working.

A cultural view of schools underlies our research approach and methodology. This means that we see a school as a culture in which participants share a set of understandings and beliefs. Using a cultural lens to examine what goes on in schools helps researchers make sense of daily interactions by examining participants' behaviors, assumptions, and values. Qualitative research uses interviewing, document analysis, and participant observation to address the question: What is happening here? Qualitative researchers observe and document what goes on in a particular setting in order to make visible the taken-for-granted details of daily interactions among people. We also participate in the setting to gain insight into "insiders'" motivations.

Qualitative researchers keep meticulous field notes on observations. We submit these field notes along with interview transcripts and site documents to rigorous analysis both during and after field work. To conduct data analysis, researchers review and code the mass of documentation, highlighting themes and patterns as well as contradictory evidence in a process of "grounded theory building."[46] When themes noted through observation are also evident in interview transcripts and/or document analysis, analytic validity is buttressed.[47]

This kind of research can aid an investigation into school climate by illuminating the varying experiences and perspectives of individuals interacting with each other. It can also provide a basis for cross-site comparisons of processes that create school climate for young adolescent girls.

A P P E N D I X   B

Overview of Data Collection

To ensure a representative sample within the parameters of this research, we selected the six schools described in this study on the basis of four factors:
• geographic location;
• diversity of girls by race/ethnicity and socioeconomic class;
• participation in school reform and/or gender equity initiatives; and
• the classification of surrounding communities as urban/
  suburban/rural settings.

For the purposes of this study, we have defined "urban," "suburban," and "rural" less in terms of census statistics than in terms of commonly observable characteristics. "Urban" refers to settings with such features as high population density, concentrated residential sections infused with commercial activity, an identifiable locus of employment in services and other sectors, a public transportation system, and often a significant minority and low-income population. Urban schools tend to have a shortage of space and material resources, in relation to an overall economic decline of U.S. cities. "Suburban" areas, in reasonable proximity to urban centers, are characterized by such features as access to city offerings from employment to entertainment, housing stock that is more spread out than in a city and often boasts single-family homes, malls that provide many goods and services, and a reliance on automobiles. Suburban schools tend to have adequate space and resources thanks to generally higher property values that increase the tax base that funds public schooling. In this report, "rural" refers to areas located well outside major urban centers. These areas tend to include towns as well as lands put to agricultural and other uses. A low population density is the norm. Automobiles are the primary mode of transportation. Rural schools may be located in towns but bus in a significant percentage of their students from outlying areas.

Five of the six are middle schools, incorporating sixth, seventh, and eighth grades; Madison is a junior high school (seventh and eighth grades).

The eight researchers, all women, are of diverse races and ethnicities and include three secondary teachers. At each school site, two or three researchers conducted the bulk of the field work, guiding "insiders"—teachers and students—who also added to the collected data.

We sought "successful" girls to participate in our field work. Our criteria for success were necessarily complex, given differing definitions of success held by different cultures inside and outside schools. While we looked at such conventional indicators as academic achievement measured by grade and test scores, we also sought the perspectives of adults in school, peers, and our own research team to identify girls who were successful in a range of ways including academically, athletically, creatively, as school and/or peer leaders, and as reflective observers of their worlds.

We also sought teachers to participate in the fieldwork. Teachers were selected by their principals, self-selected through their expressed interest in the study, and/or identified as initial contacts by colleagues in the education community.

Research teams at each site consisted of two or three "outside" researchers collaborating with at least one adult "insider" (a teacher) and several students. Inside researchers—both teachers and students—served not only as key informants but also as co-investigators who asked questions, collected and examined data, and offered interpretations from their perspectives within schools. Outside researchers utilized their extensive research training to provide insiders with direction and support. The frequency and format of insiders' meetings varied across sites: In several schools inside researchers met every few weeks to consult on their progress, while in others insiders went their separate ways, meeting irregularly.

Two rounds of fieldwork were conducted at each site. The goals of the first round included learning about the overall school context; identifying school-based as well as district and community stakeholders in the area of gender and schooling; developing relationships with adults and students who would serve as co-researchers; and identifying issues related to school reform and gender equity. Researchers spent three days on site observing events such as classes, lunch, arrival and dismissal, assemblies, faculty meetings, and extracurricular activities, and interviewing key people such as administrators, teachers involved in school reform and/or gender awareness, and girls. (See page 8 for a sample schedule.)

The goal of the second round of research was to probe deeply into school environment through the experiences of five to eight girls at each site and through interviews with teachers, parents, administrators, and community members. During this week-long site visit, researchers "shadowed" individual students for about a day each, conducting individual and focus group interviews with them and with peers and adults important to them. Shadowing provides the data to understand how actions and perceptions build over a period of time, offering a more complex picture of how individual girls experience school climate.

Individual interviews provide in-depth insights into the thoughts and world views of students and others. Focus groups made up of girls alone, boys alone, and girls and boys together provide opportunities for adolescents to explore perspectives they might not articulate one-on-one with an adult. They also provide a forum in which adolescents and adults can trade information and ideas.

Across the six sites, 52 girls participated as co-researchers and informants: These included 35 eighth graders, 15 seventh graders, and 2 sixth graders. By race/ethnicity, the breakdown was: 18 African American, 13 white, 12 Latina, 3 Native American, 3 Asian, and 3 of mixed heritage.

Of the 70 girls who participated in interviews, 34 were in the eighth grade, 23 in the seventh, and 13 in the sixth. Twenty-four were African American, 21 white, 15 Latina, 3 Native American, 3 Asian, and 4 of mixed heritage.

The focus groups involved 175 girls. Of these, 73 were eighth graders, 52 seventh graders, 40 sixth graders, and 10 recent graduates of the middle schools being studied. By race/ethnicity, the breakdown was: 61 white, 56 African American, 36 Latina, 11 Native American, 7 Asian, and 4 of mixed heritage.

See Appendix C for sample questions for girls in interviews and focus groups. These questions are culled from interview guides used by researchers in this study.

Focus groups participants also included 20 boys. Of these, 10 were eighth graders, 8 seventh graders, and 2 sixth graders. By race/ethnicity, the breakdown was: 8 African American, 5 white, 2 Latino, 1 Native American, 1 Asian, and 3 of mixed heritage.

Each student category (co-researchers, interviews, focus groups) also includes from 1 to 3 students identified as "special education" students—those judged in need of extra academic and/or emotional support. Because several of our sites are working on an "inclusion" model and do not separate special education students, this figure probably underestimates the number of students currently or formerly of this population that participated in the study.

Researchers also conducted interviews and focus groups with adults in the school communities. Of the 100 teachers who participated, 71 were female, 29 male. By race/ethnicity, the breakdown was: 65 white, 26 African American, 5 Latino, 3 Asian, and 1 of mixed heritage. See Appendix D for sample questions.

We spoke with principals at all the sites: Of these, 4 were female and 2 male. By race/ethnicity, they were: 4 white, 1 African American, and 1 Latino. See Appendix E for sample questions. We also spoke with other administrators, 2 house coordinators, 17 parents, 3 school-community liaisons, 7 counselors, 2 social workers, 1 drug prevention officer, 1 health educator, 2 nurses, 9 aides, 1 elevator operator, 1 security guard, 1 librarian, 1 reading specialist, 1 university professor, and 2 high school teachers. The adults included: whites, African Americans, Latinos, Native Americans, and Asians.

Interviews and focus groups were documented in field notes and often audiotaped and later transcribed.

In addition to the data collected by "outside" researchers, the "inside" researchers at each site also collected data. These included teacher and student dialogue journals, teacher journals, surveys of groups of youngsters and/or adults in the school, and interviews with targeted individuals including family members.

A P P E N D I X   C

Field Instruments

To ensure that researchers across the six schools asked the same kinds of questions of student and adult informants and observed the same kinds of events, we designed a set of field instruments. These included interview and focus group guides for students and adults as well as a field observation guide. Our researchers utilized these instruments not as rigid requirements but as guidelines; they tailored their questions and observations to the locale and the moment-by-moment research situation. In Appendix C, D, E, and F, we include excerpts from our research instruments, both to give readers a flavor of what we asked and looked for in this research and to provide a tool for readers' own inquiries. We hope that readers will use these guides as resources for their own research with and about girls, modifying them as needed.

Below are questions that we used with youngsters in individual interviews and/or focus groups. How and where we raised a particular question depended on what it was intended to elicit. For example, we addressed the first question—about others living in a student's household—in interview contexts to protect students' privacy, whereas the fifth question—about how students changed during middle school—was often asked in a focus group to generate collective reflection.

Sample Questions for Students

Who are the people who live in your household? What are their relationships to you, their ages, their ethnicities, their educations, and their occupations?

What do you do after school, on weekday evenings, on weekend days and evenings, on holidays, during summer vacation?

Are you into hair, clothes, TV, dancing, sports, music, boys?

Are you the same person and do you hang out with the same sort of people inside and outside of school?

How would you say you've changed from sixth grade (or elementary school) to now? Tell about how these changes happened, and what helped or hindered you along the way.

Tell us about something you've been successful at in school. It doesn't have to be academic. How did you know you were successful at this?

What do you think other people in your life see as your strengths? Why would they think that?

What do you see as your strengths? What makes you see yourself this way? How do your strengths help you already in life, and how do you think they'll help you reach your future goals?

What are some of the hardest challenges you've faced in your life? How did you deal with these?

Who has helped you to do well? Tell about how this worked, by describing a relationship or an inner direction.

Who do you hang out with? What are your friends like?

How does it feel to be (whatever race/ethnicity) as a girl in this school? How does this affect who you spend time with?

How do kids relate to each other in this house/program, girls to girls, and girls to boys?

What happens when you feel you like a boy or when he likes you?

Who lets you know often that they care about or are proud of you?

What's your favorite place to be in the community, and why? What's your favorite place to be in the school, and why? Where in the school do you not like to be, and why?

Tell us about a classroom where you feel you have learned or are learning a lot. Why is this working for you? Tell about a class where learning has been more difficult for you, and again reflect on why?

Do you ever disagree with what the teacher presents in class, and what do you do with that? Can you negotiate with teachers? What makes you comfortable to do or not do that? How do you assess the best way to move through a certain teacher's classes? How does all this impact on your learning in these classes? On your grades?

What kind of classes do you most look forward to every day? What schoolwork do you find most enjoyable and challenging? What difference do classes and activities make when you know they are aimed at making girls feel more comfortable or supported?

What is good for girls in this school? What do you call good? Is good the same for students and teachers? What would you keep the same and what would you change to make this school even better for girls?

What are your goals for the future? How do you see yourself getting there?

How do you feel about being positioned as a leader (or any other label explicitly used to describe this girl)? What do you see as characteristics of a leader? What do you like/dislike about your position in the school?

What roles were modeled for you in your family? Which have you chiseled out for yourself?

How would you describe your relationship with your mom? What are her expectations of you? How would you describe your relationship with your dad? What are his expectations of you?

Describe a time when you felt really charged up about something (big or little) and tried to make a difference. Who noticed? How did they notice? How did you feel about yourself?

What is it like to be in sixth, seventh, eighth grade? How is sixth or seventh grade different from being in elementary school? How is eighth grade different from sixth and seventh grades? What do you think high school will be like? Do you think it feels different for girls and boys? For kids of other nationalities?

What is important in this school? What do you think students, teachers, parents expect? Do you think the same things are expected from girls and boys? How do you feel about living up to what is important here? What is most important to you?

How do you let people in school know what is on your mind? Who do you feel most comfortable talking to about school issues? When you like or don't like something going on in school, who do you tell? If students want to suggest any changes in school life, what do they do?

A P P E N D I X   D

The questions listed below were taken from interview and focus group guides used with teachers in this study. The first two sets of questions—about school and community characteristics and the school's involvement with gender equity—were intended to help researchers gain an initial picture of the school's priorities and challenges particularly with regard to gender equity. Remaining sets of questions were designed to guide researchers' in-depth conversations with teachers. Readers who are teachers or interested in working with teachers might use these questions as a starting point for exploring issues of gender equity at a program, school, or district level. For example, the questions might guide a meeting of teachers interested in sharing ideas on gender and schooling.

Sample Questions for Teachers

Characteristics of the school and community

What is the school like? What is the faculty like? How has this school changed over the years? What are the kids like?

What is the community like? What are the strengths of girls in the community? What obstacles do they face? What do people in and out of school expect of girls?

How are girls' and boys' school experiences the same? Different?

School's involvement with gender equity

What are the school's priorities/vision? How do/might these translate into programs that support girls (for example, multicultural education, cooperative learning)? What programs or policies address girls' needs?

Who in the school challenges gender stereotypes? Provides other kinds of support for girls?

What places and activities in the school help girls feel comfortable and/or challenged in a positive way? Particular teachers, classes, techniques?

Is there a sex education curriculum? Policies on sexual harassment? Sexuality? Homosexuality?

What are the goals and purposes of projects and policies to support gender equity? Who started them? When? Why? What has the response been? What about support, opposition, advances, setbacks?

What would you look at to understand what works for girls here? What should we look at in greater depth?

Gender and teaching

How long have you taught? How do you think kids learn? Describe a good student. How do girls learn the same as/differently from boys?

Tell me about your experiences of gender, race, ethnicity, class issues in schools. When/why did you start thinking about gender equity as a teacher?

How do gender issues relate to/diverge from multicultural issues?

How has your practice changed over the years—in terms of curriculum? Approach to content? What has worked well for girls? What has been difficult to change?

Influence of gender concerns in the school

Who do you talk with about these issues, in what contexts, and with what kinds of responses?

How do girls inform decisions about classroom/school practice? Do they participate in initiatives from the start?

What kinds of support exist inside and outside school for work on gender issues? What are the obstacles? What are the critical issues to keep working on?

Who are key people (students, staff, parents, other stakeholders) that we should talk with? What are key places and programs to observe? Your questions?

Considering girls at your school

Think of two or three girls you have known and give a descriptive verbal snapshot of each, including her strengths, obstacles she faces, supports within and outside of school.
What do you bring to your work with girls? (Why are you interested? What is your experience?)
What strengths do girls in this school bring with them? What kinds of obstacles do they face?
What supports do girls get in the school? Outside of school?
What has worked well for girls in your classroom?
What happens in this school when girls give voice to their experiences?

A P P E N D I X   E

Researchers interviewed administrators early in the field work, seeking their perspectives on the school's overall vision, strengths, and challenges, and then again near the end of the research, taking the opportunity to reflect with administrators on what was happening in the school generally and with particular regard to gender equity. The questions listed below indicate terrain covered in both contexts, with an emphasis on the initial interview. Readers might use these questions as a resource for beginning to consider how a school can convince its district to deal with issues of gender equity.

Sample Questions for Administrators

Characteristics of the school and community

What is the school like? What is the faculty like? How has this school changed over the years?

What is the community like? What are the strengths of girls in the community? What obstacles do they face in the community? In the school?

How are girls' and boys' school experiences the same? Different?

School initiatives that work for girls

What do you think is working for girls in this school?

What are the school's priorities/vision? How do/might these translate into programs that support girls (for example, multicultural education, cooperative learning)?

What formal projects or policies address girls' needs?

Who in the school challenges gender stereotypes? Provides other kinds of support for girls?

What places and activities in the school help girls feel comfortable and/or challenged in a positive way?

Where should we look further to understand what works for girls in this school?

What would be important to change to improve girls' experiences in this school? How would you address this?

Gender and the principal

What spurred your thinking about gender issues in schools? Would you call yourself a feminist? Why?

Do you think the experience of women as administrators is different from that of male administrators? [How about experiences of African American/Latino/Caucasian administrators?]

Who do you talk with at school about gender issues, and in what contexts? Do you see your staff/curriculum/students/parents differently in light of your thinking about gender issues?

What kinds of support exist in and outside of school for work on gender equity? What are the obstacles? What kinds of issues come up around sexuality education, sexual harassment, homosexuality?

Who are the key people (students, staff, parents, other stakeholders) that we should talk with? Key places and programs to observe? Your questions?

A P P E N D I X F

Field Guides

We used three instruments to guide work in the field to make sure we got vital information and addressed issues across sites for viable analysis and writing. Our intent was to allow researchers optimal freedom in writing up field notes while also making sure we were not left with any significant gaps in what we knew across sites.

1. We created a chart for researchers to fill out that gave us, in a quick-read format, the nuts and bolts of the sites:

Place: State/city/town. School district name and size. School name, grades, size. Urban/rural/suburban. Student demographics (how many, gender/race, class breakdown, special populations, etc.).

Researchers: Names of outside researchers, dates of visits. Names of teacher-researchers and student-researchers, identified by position in school, grade level, race, gender, and other relevant characteristics.

Key players: Names and positions of other key people in the school and community, such as administrators, counselor, nurse, secretary, parent contact person, school board member, etc.

Programs: Curricular and extracurricular activities in place or in process to support girls. Other innovative initiatives.

Policies: Note relevant school policies, for example, on sexual harassment, diversity.

2. We drew up a checklist of questions and issues that researchers made sure they had attended to before leaving the site after first- and second-round visits. The checklist indicated areas that needed more focus on the second visit.

Context: What are the characteristics of the community in which this school is situated? What is the school known for in the community? Where are parents and other community members visible in the life of the school? What happened up to and including your initial entry into this school—note conversations, written exchanges, concerns/hopes/questions before entry. What happened as you entered the building: for example, what did you see, who did you meet, how did you get oriented?

Mapping the site: Place and time: Describe the physical space. Name and describe key places in this school, especially for girls, for example, public spaces, offices, classrooms, bathrooms, outdoor space, lunchroom, etc. Describe how space and time are organized. For example, are there sub-units such as houses or teams? Where are these located? How is the school day structured for students and teachers? How does this vary across individuals, and over a week, or the year? What are important times/places to know about for girls, for example, "locker talk" before homeroom?

Key people: Identify staff, students, administrators, aides, parents, community members and any other stakeholders key to "school climate for girls." Identify person's position in relation to school/community and the group(s) they might "represent" (for example, social groups, grade, house, discipline). Include descriptions of these people (how they look, what they say/do, who they hang out with), especially in relation to gender issues. What are their perspectives on girls' experiences and gender issues in school?

Contextual factors: Describe what this school is doing to support girls and to get gender issues addressed, for example, curricular and extracurricular activities and less formal goings-on. Include perspectives of various key players, and connect with places and times where possible. Note other relevant influences, such as teacher development workshops, AAUW findings, community organizations, political organizations, women's movement, literature, etc.

Classroom/shadow guide: How do students interact with each other and with the teacher as they enter and leave class? During class? What is the physical environment of the classroom? What's the content of the lesson, and how is it approached in terms of materials and pedagogy? In nonclassroom settings such as lunchroom or playground, what are setting and atmosphere like? How do students interact with each other and with adults?

Reflections and plans: Include new ways that you're coming to understand girls' experiences here, as well as your questions, concerns, and plans for ongoing research at this site. What issues still need to be addressed? Addressed again?

3. We specified categories for researchers to use when organizing field notes following first- and second-round visits:

- People in the school, for example, teacher expectations, teaching styles, teacher/student interactions that influence girls' opportunities and achievements.
- Places in the school, including public spaces such as offices and classrooms and private spaces such as bathrooms and counselors' offices.
- Program and curriculum, for example, instruction, guidance programs, extracurricular activities.
- Policies, for example, on diversity, hiring, harassment, and traditional norms.
- Priorities/vision of the school.

A   P   P   E   N   D   I   X   G

Research Calendar

September - October 1994	Finalized all school sites. Established contact with teacher-researcher(s). Held researcher meeting to establish cross-site questions, objectives, and methodologies. Piloted three-day site visit in one or two schools.
November 1994	Conducted three-day site visits in all schools.
December 1994	Held researcher meeting to look at data across sites; this informed upcoming intensive visits.
January 1995	Conducted week-long site visits in all schools.
February - March 1995	Met with researchers. Analyzed data.
April 1995	Videotaped. Analyzed data.
May - June 1995	Analyzed data and drafted report.

1. Janie Ward, "High Self-Esteem/Low Achievement: The AAUW Findings on Black Girls Growing Up," paper presented at a symposium on the psychology of girls and the culture of schools (Temple University, Philadelphia, 1993).

   T. Robinson and Janie Ward, "'A Belief in Self Far Greater Than Anyone's Disbelief': Cultivating Resistance Among African American Female Adolescents," in *Women, Girls & Psychotherapy: Reframing Resistance*, Carol Gilligan, Annie G. Rogers, and Deborah L. Tolman, eds. (New York: Harrington Park Press, 1991): 87-103.

   Patricia Williams, *The Alchemy of Race and Rights* (Cambridge, Mass.: Harvard University Press, 1991).

2. Lyn Brown and Carol Gilligan, *Meeting at the Crossroads: Women's Psychology and Girls' Development* (New York: Ballantine Books, 1992).

3. Anne C. Lewis, *Gaining Ground: The Highs and Lows of Urban Middle School Reform 1989-1991* (New York: The Edna McConnell Clark Foundation, Fall 1991).

   Gayle Dorman and Anne Wheelock, *Before It's Too Late: Dropout Prevention in the Middle Grades* (Carrboro, N.C.: Center for Early Adolescence, 1988).

   California State Department of Education, *Caught in the Middle: Educational Reform for Young Adolescents in California Public Schools* (1987).

   Joyce Epstein and D. J. MacIver, *Education in the Middle Grades, National Practices and Trends* (Baltimore: National Middle School Association, 1990).

   The Edna McConnell Clark Foundation, *Making It in the Middle: The Why and How of Excellent Schools for Young Urban Adolescents* (Anne C. Lewis, ed., 1990).

4. Carol Gilligan, "Women's Psychological Development: Implications for Psychotherapy," in *Women, Girls & Psychotherapy: Reframing Resistance*, Carol Gilligan, Annie G. Rogers, and D. L. Tolman, eds. (New York: Harrington Park Press, 1991): 5-31.

   Brown and Gilligan, *Meeting at the Crossroads*.

   Robinson and Ward, "'A Belief in Self Far Greater Than Anyone's Disbelief.'"

   Mary Pipher, *Reviving Ophelia: Saving the Souls of Adolescent Girls* (New York: Putnam, 1994).

5. *The AAUW Report: How Schools Shortchange Girls*, researched by the Wellesley College Center for Research on Women (Washington, D.C.: American Association of University Women Educational Foundation, 1992): 90-93.

6. Myra Sadker and David Sadker, *Failing at Fairness: How America's Schools Cheat Girls* (New York: Charles Scribner's Sons, 1994).

7. Peggy Orenstein, *SchoolGirls: Young Women, Self-Esteem and the Confidence Gap* (New York: Doubleday, 1994).

8. AAUW Educational Foundation, *Growing Smart: What's Working for Girls in School: Executive Summary and Action Guide*, researched by Sunny Hansen, Joyce Walker, and Barbara Flom (Washington, D.C.: American Association of University Women Educational Foundation, 1995): 3-4.

9. *The AAUW Report: How Schools Shortchange Girls.*

   AAUW Educational Foundation, *Growing Smart.*

10. Ibid.

    Gilligan, "Women's Psychological Development."

    Brown and Gilligan, *Meeting at the Crossroads.*

    Robinson and Ward, "'A Belief in Self Far Greater Than Anyone's Disbelief.'"

    Ardy Bowker, *Sisters in the Blood: The Education of Women in Native America* (Newton, Mass.: WEEA Publishing Center, 1993).

    Barrie Thorne, *Gender Play* (New Brunswick, N.J.: Rutgers University Press, 1993).

    Michelle Fine, "Sexuality, Schooling, and Adolescent Females: The Missing Discourse of Desire," in *Beyond Silenced Voices: Class, Race, and Gender in United States Schools,* Lois Weis and Michelle Fine, eds. (New York: State University of New York Press, 1993).

    Pat Macpherson and Michelle Fine, "Hungry for Us: Adolescent Girls and Adult Women Negotiating Territories of Race, Gender, Class, and Difference," *Feminism and Psychology* 5, no. 2. (May 1995): 181-200.

    AAUW Educational Foundation, *Growing Smart.*

    Pipher, *Reviving Ophelia.*

11. Thorne, *Gender Play.*

12. R. W. Connell, "Disruptions: Improper Masculinities and Schooling," in *Beyond Silenced Voices: Class, Race, and Gender in United States Schools,* Lois Weis and Michelle Fine, eds., (New York: State University of New York Press, 1993): 191-208.

13. Patty Lather, *Getting Smart: Feminist Research and Pedagogy Within the Postmodern* (New York: Routledge, 1991).

    Donna Haraway, "Situated Knowledges: The Science Question in Feminism and the Privilege of Partial Perspective," *Feminist Studies* 14, no. 3. (1988): 575-599.

14. Frederick Erickson, "Qualitative Methods in Research on Teaching," in M. C. Wittrock, ed., *Handbook of Research on Teaching,* 3rd ed. (New York: MacMillan, 1986).

15. Jolley Christman, "Working in the Field as the Female Friend," *Anthropology and Education Quarterly* 19, no. 2 (1988): 70-85.

    Judith Goetz and Linda Grant, "Conceptual Approaches to Studying Gender in Education," *Anthropology and Education Quarterly* 19, no. 2 (1988): 182-196.

    Dorothy Smith, "Writing Women's Experience Into Social Science," *Feminism and Psychology* 1, no. 1 (1991): 155-169.

16. *The AAUW Report: How Schools Shortchange Girls.*

17. Thorne, *Gender Play:* 3.

18. Gilligan, "Women's Psychological Development."

    Annie Rogers, "Voice, Play, and a Practice of Ordinary Courage in Girls' and Women's Lives," *Harvard Educational Review* 63, no. 3 (1993): 265-295.

    Emily Hancock, *The Girl Within* (New York: Fawcett Columbia, 1989).

    Ward, "High Self-Esteem/Low Achievement."

19. Gilligan, "Women's Psychological Development."

    Brown and Gilligan, *Meeting at the Crossroads*: 1.

20. Gilligan, "Women's Psychological Development": 14.

21. Robinson and Ward, "'A Belief in Self Far Greater Than Anyone's Disbelief'": 88.

22. Bowker, *Sisters in the Blood*: 260.

23. Robinson and Ward, "'A Belief in Self Far Greater Than Anyone's Disbelief'": 89.

24. Donna Eder with Katherine Colleen Evans and Stephen Parker, *School Talk: Gender and Adolescent Culture* (New Brunswick, N. J.: Rutgers University Press, 1995).

    Roberta Tovey, "A Narrowly Gender-Based Model of Learning May End Up Cheating All Students," *Harvard Education Review Newsletter*, July-August, 1995: 3-5. Tovey describes work by Gilligan and her colleagues in which white and African American working-class girls share speaking styles.

25. Sadker and Sadker, *Failing at Fairness*.

26. Brown and Gilligan, *Meeting at the Crossroads*: 4.

27. Selase Williams, "Classroom Use of African American Language: Educational Tool or Social Weapon?" in *Empowerment Through Multicultural Education*, Christine Sleeter, ed. (New York: State University of New York Press, 1991).

28. AAUW Educational Foundation, *Growing Smart*.

29. This adds an interesting dimension to Gilligan's research at an elite girls' school, where adult women must struggle to retain their connection with adolescent girls. Carol Gilligan, "Joining the Resistance: Psychology, Politics, Girls and Women," in *Beyond Silenced Voices*, Lois Weis and Michelle Fine, eds. (New York: State University of New York Press, 1993).

30. Howard Gardner, *Frames of Mind: The Theory of Multiple Intelligences* (New York: Basic Books, 1983).

31. *National Council of Teachers of Mathematics, Curriculum and Evaluation Standards for School Mathematics* (Reston, Va., 1989).

32. Task Force on Education of Young Adolescents, *Turning Points: Preparing America's Youth for the 21st Century* (Washington, D.C.: Carnegie Council on Adolescent Development, 1989).

    Gisela Konopka, "Requirements for Healthy Development of Adolescent Youth," *Adolescence*, 31 (1973).

    Karen J. Pittman, and Michele Cahill, *A New Vision: Promoting Youth Development*, commissioned paper #3 (Washington, D.C.: Academy for Educational Development, 1991).

33. National Council of Teachers of Mathematics, *Curriculum and Evaluation Standards for School Mathematics* (Reston, Va., 1989).

34. Peggy McIntosh, *Interactive Phases of Curricular Re-Vision: A Feminist Perspective*, Working Paper no. 124 (Wellesley, Mass.: Wellesley College Center for Research on Women, 1983).

    Emily Style, *Multicultural Education and Me: The Philosophy and the Process, Putting Product in Its Place* (Madison, Wisc.: Teacher Corps Associates, University of Wisconsin, 1982).

35. Task Force on Education of Young Adolescents, *Turning Points*, 1989.

36. AAUW Educational Foundation, *Growing Smart*.

37. Deborah Meier, *The Power of Their Ideas: Lessons for America From a Small School in Harlem* (Boston: Houghton Mifflin Company, 1993).

    Warren L. Saunders, "The Constructivist Perspective: Implications and Teaching Strategies for Science," *School Science and Mathematics* 92, no. 3 (1992).

    Theodore R. Sizer, *Horace's School: Redesigning the American High School* (Boston: Houghton Mifflin Company, 1993).

    Diane R. Waff, "Girl Talk: Creating Community Through Social Exchange," in *Chartering Urban School Reform: Reflections on Public High Schools in the Midst of Change*, Michelle Fine, ed. (New York: Teachers College Press, 1994): 192-203.

    Jody Cohen, "'Now Everybody Want to Dance': Making Change in an Urban Charter," in *Chartering Urban School Reform: Reflections on Public High Schools in the Midst of Change*, Michelle Fine, ed. (New York: Teachers College Press, 1994): 192-203.

38. AAUW Educational Foundation, *Growing Smart*.

39. Ibid.: 11.

40. Ibid.

41. Ibid.

42. Brown and Gilligan, *Meeting at the Crossroads*.

    Deborah L. Tolman, "Adolescent Girls, Women and Sexuality: Discerning Dilemmas of Desire," in *Women, Girls and Psychotherapy*, Carol Gilligan, Annie G. Rogers, Deborah L. Tolman, eds. (New York: Harrington Park Press, 1991).

43. Marilyn Cochran-Smith and Susan Lytle, *Inside/Outside: Teacher Research and Knowledge* (New York: Teachers College Press, 1993).

44. AAUW Educational Foundation, *Growing Smart*.

45. Gardner, *Frames of Mind*.

46. Barney Glaser and Anselm Strauss, *The Discovery of Grounded Theory: Strategies for Qualitative Research* (Chicago: Aldine, 1967).

47. Frederick Erickson, "Qualitative Methods in Research on Teaching."

Jody C. Cohen

Jody C. Cohen is a director of Research for Action, Inc., a nonprofit educational research and evaluation group in Philadelphia. She is the author of "'Now Everybody Want to Dance': Making Change in an Urban Charter," in *Chartering Urban School Reform* (Teachers College Press, 1994), "Constructing Race at an Urban High School: 'In Their Minds, Their Mouths, Their Hearts'" in *Beyond Silenced Voices: Class, Race, and Gender in United States Schools* (SUNY Press, 1993), and co-author of "Growing Smaller: Three Tasks of High School Restructuring" in *Urban Education* (March 1996). Her research and evaluation work includes participatory inquiry with teachers, parents, students, and administrators. A former teacher, she earned her doctorate with distinction from the University of Pennsylvania Graduate School of Education.

Sukey Blanc

Sukey Blanc is a research associate for Research for Action, Inc., and co-author of many reports including, "An Evaluation of the New York City Mathematics Project" (Lehman College, CUNY, 1995) and "I'm No Longer Afraid to Say I Don't Know: Becoming Scientists/Becoming Leaders" (Research for Action, 1994). She has also presented at many conferences about her work on adolescent girls. A former teacher, she has a master's degree in education from Temple University, a master's degree in linguistics from the University of Pennsylvania, and is a doctoral candidate in anthropology at Temple University. In 1993 she received an American Fellowship from the AAUW Educational Foundation for her dissertation on middle school girls, "She Thinks She's Bad: An Ethnographic Study of Difference and Identity Among Young Adolescent Girls."

Jolley Bruce Christman

Jolley Bruce Christman is president of Research for Action, Inc., and author of numerous school reform evaluation projects, including "The Five School Study: Restructuring Urban High Schools," funded by the Pew Charitable Trusts. She also writes in the areas of feminist research and participatory approaches to evaluation. A former teacher, she received her doctorate with distinction from the University of Pennsylvania. In 1992 she received the Ethnographic Evaluation Award for Excellence from the American Anthropological Association for her research on the impact of the Philadelphia Education Fund during its first five years.

Diane C. Brown

Diane C. Brown is a language arts and program support teacher at Gillespie Middle School in Philadelphia. She is completing work at Lehigh University for her elementary/secondary principal certification. She has been a leader in several reform programs including the Pennsylvania Humanities Council's GATE program and the Gratz Project. She received her master's degree magna cum laude from St. John's College and did advanced work at Harvard School of Education, Wilkes, and Drexel Universities.

Michele Jean Sims

Michele Jean Sims is a doctoral candidate in reading/writing/literacy at the University of Pennsylvania. Formerly, she taught in New York City and Philadelphia. In Philadelphia she was a reading/language arts teacher at the Jay Cooke Middle School, where she participated in an ungraded, interdisciplinary program for at-risk students. Committed to issues of literacy, race, and gender, she has been a co-facilitator of the Middle School Students At Risk Cluster Initiative and the Philadelphia Writing Project. She is interested in teacher inquiry as professional development, especially in middle schools. She received a master's degree in developmental and remedial reading from the City University of New York.

Research Planning Team

Ruth Ann Burns is vice president of the Educational Resources Center of Thirteen/WNET, the nation's flagship public television station. She is responsible for the station's activities in education, technology, and new media. Prior to her public television work, she was a senior research and program associate at the Eagleton Institute of Politics at Rutgers University.

Michelle Fine is professor of psychology and social psychology in the Personality Program CUNY/Graduate Center. Her many books include *Chartering Urban School Reform: Reflections on Public High School in the Midst of Change* (Teachers College Press, 1994) and *Beyond Silenced Voices: Class, Race and Gender in United States Schools* (CUNY Press, 1993) with L. Weis. For her book *Framing Dropouts: Notes on the Politics of an Urban High School* (CUNY Press, 1991) she received the Distinguished Book Award from the Society for Research on Adolescence.

Angela Ginorio is director of the University of Washington's Northwest Center for Research on Women. She is a co-editor of *The Equity Equation: Fostering the Advancement of Women in the Sciences, Mathematics, and Engineering* (Jossey Bass, 1996). She is chair of the Committee on Women in Psychology of the American Psychological Association and was an adviser for *Hostile Hallways: The AAUW Survey on Sexual Harassment in America's Schools* (AAUW Educational Foundation, 1993).

Ginny Gong is an administrator with the Department of Human Relations of Montgomery County Public Schools in Maryland. A former mathematics teacher, she is the immediate past president of the Organization of Chinese Americans, a civil rights advocacy group with 40 chapters nationwide.

Luke Henderson is president of Research in Values and Attitudes (RIVA) Market Research, Inc., a qualitative market research organization, in Bethesda, Maryland. He moderates focus groups and conducts training workshops and seminars. He has clients in government, education, health, media, finance, and public policy.

Anthony T. Podesta is president of Podesta Associates, a public policy, government relations, and public affairs firm. He is founding president of People for the American Way, a national nonpartisan citizens' organization designed to protect constitutional liberties. His op-ed pieces have appeared in the *New York Times*, the *Washington Post*, and the *Los Angeles Times*.

Arensa Strange is a 1992-93 AAUW Educational Foundation Eleanor Roosevelt Teacher Fellow and a recipient of a 1995 AAUW Educational Foundation Community Action Grant. Since 1974 she has taught mathematics at the Model Secondary School for the Deaf at Gallaudet University in Washington, DC. She has received the Washington Post Agnes Meyer Outstanding Teacher Award and the Presidential Award for Excellence in Teaching Mathematics and Science.

Barrie Thorne is professor of sociology and women's studies at the University of California at Berkeley. She is a member of the MacArthur Foundation Research Network on Successful Pathways Through Middle Childhood and is the author of *Gender Play: Girls and Boys in School* (Rutgers University Press, 1993) and co-editor of *Language, Gender, and Society* (Newbury House, 1983).

Alexandra Wagner is a second-year student at Brown University. She was her class salutatorian at Woodrow Wilson High School in Washington, DC, from which she graduated in 1995.

Janie Victoria Ward is an associate professor in the Department of Education and Human Services at Simmons College in Boston. She is a past recipient of a Rockefeller Foundation Postdoctoral Research Fellowship at the Center for the Study of Black Literature and Culture, University of Pennsylvania. She is a co-editor with Carol Gilligan and Jill Taylor of *Mapping the Moral Domain: A Contribution of Women's Thinking to Psychological Theory and Education* (Harvard University Press, 1988).

INDEX

RESOURCES: THE AAUW EQUITY LIBRARY

Groundbreaking Works on Gender Bias in Education

Girls in the Middle: Working to Succeed in School
Engaging study of middle school girls and the strategies they use to meet the challenges of adolescence. Report links girls' success to school reforms like team teaching and cooperative learning, especially where these are used to address gender issues. 128 pages/1996.
$12.95 AAUW members /$14.95 nonmembers.

Girls in the Middle: Working to Succeed in School Video
An absorbing look at girls in three middle schools and the strategies they use to meet challenges in their daily lives. Includes video guide with discussion questions, program resources, and action strategies.
VHS format/26 minutes/1996.
$19.95 AAUW members /$24.95 nonmembers.

Growing Smart: What's Working for Girls in School Executive Summary and Action Guide
Illustrated summary of academic report identifying themes and approaches that promote girls' achievement and healthy development. Based on review of more than 500 studies and reports. Includes action strategies; program resource list; and firsthand accounts of some program participants. 60 pages/1995.
$10.95 AAUW members/$12.95 nonmembers.

Girls Can! Community Coalitions Resource Manual
Comprehensive guide for organizations and individuals seeking to launch and sustain community-based programs for girls. Offers tips for building coalitions, recruiting volunteers, planning projects, raising funds, and gaining media attention. Includes contact information for more than 200 national and grassroots organizations. 167 pages/1996.
$10.95 AAUW members/$12.95 nonmembers.

Girls Can! Video
Complement to *Shortchanging Girls, Shortchanging America*. An inspirational look at programs around the country that are making a difference in fighting gender bias in schools.
VHS format/16 minutes/1995.
$19.95 AAUW members/$24.95 nonmembers.

AAUW Issue Briefs
Set of five briefs explores gender equity issues including treatment of students, educator training, the curriculum, college admissions testing, and education and training. 1990-1995.
$7.95 AAUW members/$9.95 nonmembers.

How Schools Shortchange Girls: The AAUW Report
Marlowe paperback edition, 1995. A startling examination of how girls are disadvantaged in America's schools, grades K-12. Includes recommendations for educators and policymakers as well as concrete strategies for change. 240 pages.
$11.95 AAUW members/$12.95 nonmembers.

The AAUW Report Executive Summary
Overview of *How Schools Shortchange Girls* research, with recommendations for educators and policymakers. 8 pages/1992.
$6.95 AAUW members/$8.95 nonmembers.

Hostile Hallways: The AAUW Survey on Sexual Harassment in America's Schools
The first national study of sexual harassment in school, based on the experiences of 1,632 students in grades 8 through 11. Gender and ethnic/racial (African American, Hispanic, and white) data breakdowns included. Commissioned by the AAUW Educational Foundation and conducted by Louis Harris and Associates. 28 pages/1993.
$8.95 AAUW members/$11.95 nonmembers.

SchoolGirls: Young Women, Self-Esteem, and the Confidence Gap
Doubleday, 1994. Riveting book by journalist Peggy Orenstein in association with AAUW shows how girls in two racially and economically diverse California communities suffer the painful plunge in self-esteem documented in *Shortchanging Girls, Shortchanging America*. 384 pages.
$18.95 AAUW members/$21.95 nonmembers.

Shortchanging Girls, Shortchanging America Executive Summary
Summary of the 1991 poll that assesses self-esteem, educational experiences, and career aspirations of girls and boys ages 9-15. Revised edition reviews poll's impact, offers action strategies, and highlights survey results with charts and graphs. 20 pages/1994.
$8.95 AAUW members/$11.95 nonmembers.

Shortchanging Girls, Shortchanging America Video
A dramatic look at the inequities girls face in school. Features education experts and public policy leaders, AAUW poll results, and the compelling voices and faces of American girls.
VHS format/15 minutes/1991.
$19.95 AAUW members/$24.95 nonmembers.

Help Make a Difference for Today's Girls...and Tomorrow's Leaders

Become part of the American Association of University Women, representing 150,000 college graduates, and help promote education and equity for women and girls. You can add your voice as a member-at-large or work on critical issues in one of AAUW's more than 1,600 local branches. For further membership information, write: AAUW Membership, Dept. G, 1111 Sixteenth St. N.W., Washington, DC 20036-4873.

The AAUW Educational Foundation, a not-for-profit 501(c)(3) organization, provides funds to advance education, research, and self-development for women, and to foster equity and positive societal change. Your dollars support research, community action projects, and fellowships for women scholars and teachers. Send contributions to: AAUW Educational Foundation, Dept. 363, 1111 Sixteenth St. N.W., Washington, DC 20036-4873.

AAUW Resources Order Form

Name _____

Address _____

City/State/Zip _____

Daytime phone (_____) _____

AAUW membership # (if applicable) _____

Item	Circle Price Member/Nonmember	Quantity	Total
Girls in the Middle: Working to Succeed in School	$12.95/$14.95	_____	_____
Girls in the Middle Video	$19.95/$24.95	_____	_____
Growing Smart Executive Summary and Action Guide	$10.95/$12.95	_____	_____
Girls Can! Community Coalitions Resource Manual	$10.95/$12.95	_____	_____
Girls Can! Video	$19.95/$24.95	_____	_____
AAUW Issue Briefs 5-Pack	$7.95/$9.95	_____	_____
How Schools Shortchange Girls	$11.95/$12.95	_____	_____
How Schools Shortchange Girls Executive Summary	$6.95/$8.95	_____	_____
Hostile Hallways	$8.95/$11.95	_____	_____
SchoolGirls	$18.95/$21.95	_____	_____
Shortchanging Girls Executive Summary	$8.95/$11.95	_____	_____
Shortchanging Girls Video	$19.95/$24.95	_____	_____
		Subtotal:	_____
	Tax *(DC, MD residents only)*:		_____
International Order Surcharge *(25% of subtotal above)*:			_____
		Shipping/Handling:	$4.00
AAUW Membership-at-Large	$35	_____	_____
		TOTAL ORDER:	_____

For bulk pricing on orders of 10 or more, call 800/225-9998 ext. 363.
Please make check or money order payable in U.S. currency to AAUW. Do not send cash.
Credit cards are accepted for orders of $10 or more.

☐ MasterCard ☐ Visa Card #__ __ __ __ - __ __ __ __ - __ __ __ __ - __ __ __ __ Expiration _____

Name on card _____

Cardholder signature _____

SATISFACTION GUARANTEED: If you are not completely satisfied with your purchase, please return it within 90 days for exchange, credit, or refund. Videos are returnable only if defective, and for replacement only.

☐ Please send me information on joining an AAUW branch in my area (dues vary by branch).
☐ I'd like to join as a member-at-large. Enclosed is $35. (Fill in education information below.)

_____   _____   _____
College/University   State/Campus   Year/Degree

FOR MAIL ORDERS, SEND THIS FORM TO:
AAUW Sales Office
Dept. 363
P.O. Box 251
Annapolis Junction, MD 20701-0251

FOR TELEPHONE ORDERS, CALL:
800/225-9998 ext. 363

CODE: D97ROS